ART AND HISTORY OF
JERUSALEM

THE HOLY CITY - 3000 YEARS

BONECHI & STEIMATZKY

CONTENTS

History of Jerusalem

THE ORIGINS AND THE EARLIEST WRITTEN EVIDENCE

*A*lthough the origins of Jerusalem are shrouded in the mists of time, on the basis of archeological findings scholars have set the dawn of the third millennium as the beginning of its history. A tribe of Canaanites settled on the heights 770 meters above sea level, between the valley of Kidron on the east and the valley the Greeks were later to call Tyropoeon on the west; south of the settlement these two valleys merged into the valley of Hinnom. Even though modest in size, the site offered natural defenses and the presence of a spring (Gihon Spring), which must have influenced the Canaanites decision to settle here.

Written evidence does not appear until the beginning of the next millennium when Jerusalem is mentioned in the Egyptian "Execration Texts" of the nineteenth century B.C. At the time semi-nomadic tribes lived in the land of Canaan and the few city-states in the area acted as buffers between the two great powers of the time: the empire of the Egyptian Pharaohs to the south, that of the Assyrians to the north. These city-states, each with its own king, were vassals of one or the other of these empires depending on how the pendulum swung. Once conquered, they became allies of the victor to whom they paid tributes. They were also ready to "pass to the enemy" as soon as they thought the winds of victory were veering in the other direction. The ruling power thus was never certain of what would happen on the morrow. In an attempt to bring a halt to such defections, the Egyptians turned to magic: breaking a vase, a figure, or a tablet on which the name of a city was inscribed was an omen of its destruction. These "Execration Texts" served as psychological deterrents for the vassals who were all too ready to rebel. Jerusalem appears in them as Urushamen (Urusalem in the Akkadian language); the name means "the foundation of the (city) of the (god) Shalem" and bears witness to the religious importance of the site in earliest times. Shalem was in fact the local divinity.

Shalem is also the name by which Jerusalem first appears in the Bible, when Abraham, who came from Ur of Chaldea, arrived here with his wife Sarah, around 1700 B.C. and met "Melchizedek king of Shalem" who was also the "priest of the most high God" (Genesis 14, 18). The site is mentioned once more in Genesis 22, 2, where the Eternal orders Abraham to go to Mount Moriah, north of the original settlement, and sacrifice his son Isaac.

The seventeenth and sixteenth centuries B.C. witnessed the invasion from the north of the powerful Hyksos peoples, with their horse-drawn war chariots. They overran and subjugated not only the land of Canaan but also Egypt, which succeeded in freeing itself only after a hundred and fifty years of domination. At the beginning of the fourteenth century B.C., under Amenophis III, Egypt had once more acquired hegemony over Canaan and pushed northwards to subjugate the lands of Syria.

Some of the tablets found in El Amarna in 1891-92 contained the correspondence between the Pharaohs Amenophis III and Amenophis IV-Akhenaton and the vassals of Egypt. Jerusalem is mentioned again, although no longer as a city in the "Execration Texts". The words are now those of the King himself as he asks the Pharaohs for aid, defending himself from accusations of rebellion brought up by another nearby king, and accusing him in turn of rebellion.

THE TRIBES OF ISRAEL CONQUER THE LAND OF CANAAN

*O*nce more the veil of silence falls; the name appears anew in the Bible when, between the 13th and 12th centuries B.C., Adonizedek, King of Jerusalem (now no longer Shalem), is included in the list of Kings defeated by Joshua (Joshua, 10), the commander who during the exodus from Egypt prevailed over the Amalekites. He led the people of Israel towards the Promised Land after the death of Moses, and took the city of Jericho. Even so Jerusalem remained in the hands of its inhabitants, the Jebusites, a people whose origins are still unknown and of whom mention is to be found only in the Bible. The reason Joshua did not try to take over the city was probably because the Philistines landed on the coast just about the time that he was conquering the hilly ranges of the land of Canaan. One of the "peoples of the sea", they seem to have come from the Aegean islands, more specifically Crete. Driven back by Ramses III when they attempted to land in Egypt, the Philistines had settled as vassals of the Pharaoh in the southern part of the region, on the borders with Egypt; but it was not long before they moved onto the coastal plains and into the interior, although still as vassals of the Pharaoh. These movements of the Philistines led to clashes with the tribes of Israel who had occupied the uplands. The times were not easy for the people of Israel. After centuries of enslavement, years of wandering in the desert and struggles with the peoples met along their way to the Promised Land, the twelve tribes were also at odds with each other. They were adapting themselves to an independent and sedentary way of life as farmers which signified a radical change in their life-style. This was not the time to go to war against the Jebusites, who remained in Jerusalem for another 250 years, constituting an enclave in the lands of the Israelites; however the tribes of Benjamin and Judah had settled around the city.

The danger the Philistines represented contributed

3

Scale model of Jerusalem in the era of Herod (scale 1:50) from the Holyland Hotel. A detail with King David's Tomb, the Temple and the Antonia Fortress.

to bonding the twelve tribes together and they finally accepted the monarchy, which was contrary to the tradition of Israel. Saul was the first king of Israel: during his reign, at the end of the second millennium B.C., the Philistines were defeated several times, and finally prevailed in the battle of Ghilboa, in which Saul himself died.

JERUSALEM IN THE TIME OF DAVID

*T*he task of conquering the Philistines and occupying Zion, the Jebusite fort on Mount Moriah, fell to Saul's successor, David (1006-973 B.C.). He left the Jebusites free to live in Jerusalem, and turned the city into the capital of the kingdom of Israel: "And David dwelt in the fort and called it 'the city of David'. And David built round about" (2 Samuel 5,9). "And Hiram king of Tyre sent messengers to David, and cedar trees and carpenters, and masons and they built David a house" (2 Samuel 5, 11).
In the time of David the city was elongated in form

and reached south to the Pool of Shiloah and north to about 220 meters from the present south wall of Jerusalem; on the east and west it was bordered by the valleys of Kidron and Tyropoeon. David did more than make Jerusalem the capital of a kingdom, he also made it the religious center for all of Israel, transporting the Ark of the Covenant there and setting it under a tent. The Ark contained the Tablets of the Law, testimony of the pact between God and Israel. It was his successor, Solomon, who built the Temple to house the Ark.
After David, Jerusalem, Zion and Israel were to be synonymous.

SOLOMON AND THE BUILDING OF THE TEMPLE

*U*nder Solomon (973-933 B.C.), Jerusalem was the capital of a prosperous and peaceful realm, allied with Egypt (Solomon took Pharaoh's daughter as a wife) and Tyre; the copper mines in the Negev desert began to be exploited and trade with the neighboring countries flourished.
The building boom in Jerusalem reflected the continuous development of its economy. The monumental works achieved at this time were visible evidence of its importance as an economic, political and religious capital.
The Bible describes in detail the preparations for the construction of the Temple of the Lord on the threshing floor of Araunah (or Ornan) the Jebusite, previously acquired by David for the building of an altar. The land was north of the city on Mount Moriah, where Abraham had gone to sacrifice Isaac. Since Hiram of Tyre supplied many laborers, in addition to cedar and cypress wood, it is not surprising that the plan and many furnishings recall similar buildings in Syria.
The Temple, built on a podium, was rectangular in form, had its entrance facing east and consisted of a porch (ulam), a courtyard called Holy Place (hekal), and the Holy of Holies (devir). The entire length, including the porch (5 meters), the hekal (20 meters), and the devir (10 meters) was 35 meters, while it was 10 meters wide. The Holy of Holies (devir) was cube-shaped.
In the hekal were 10 bronze basins on the same number of bases mounted on wheels, 5 on the right and 5 on the left, for the purification of the sacrificial offerings; the "molten sea", located to the southeast, for the ablutions of the priests (it was a large basin 5 meters in diameter, supported by twelve bronze oxen, which faced, three each, towards the cardinal directions); and the square copper altar, 5 meters high and 10 on each side. Before the devir rose two pillars of bronze, called Jachin and Boaz, 9 meters high, at the top of which were capitals of lily work containing a sphere inside.
The devir was covered with cedar wood and overlaid with gold and contained the Holy Ark and two gilded cherubim. This room, illuminated only by a lamp, was accessible solely to the High Priest on the Day of Atonement (Yom Ha-Kippurim).
On the south side of the Temple base was the complex of buildings including the magnificent royal Palace, the "house of the daughter of the Pharaoh", the columned Porch, the Porch of the Throne where the King administered justice and the "House of the

Forest of Lebanon", so called because it had forty-five columns in cedar of Lebanon.
With the construction of the temple, Jerusalem was definitively consecrated as the religious center of Israel.

JERUSALEM THE CAPITAL OF THE KINGDOM OF JUDAH

A long period of decadence set in after the death of Solomon. During the reign of Rehoboam, his son, the tribes of the north rebelled against the dynasty of David. The result was the formation of two states which were often at war with each other: the Kingdom of Israel to the north with Samaria as its capital, and that of Judah to the south with Jerusalem as capital. During this period Jerusalem was also attacked and plundered by the Pharaoh Sheshonq.
In 772 B.C. Israel and its capital fell into the hands of the Assyrians who deported more than twenty thousand inhabitants. The Kingdom of Judah with its capital Jerusalem and the Temple remained the sole guardian of the hopes of the people of Israel.
A period of particular importance in the history of Jerusalem began at this point. On the one hand the King Hezekiah strengthened the defenses of the city in preparation for attacks by the Assyrians, on the other the prophet Isaiah exhorted men to persevere in the Law of the Lord and fortify their souls to withstand the enemy. In preparation for siege, Hezekiah had a tunnel cut into the living rock to bring water from Gihon Spring, which was outside the walls, into the city where it was collected in the Pool of Siloa.
When the powerful army of the Assyrian King Sennacherib (705-681 B.C.) launched its attack on the Kingdom of Judah, the only city to escape siege was Jerusalem. It seemed a miracle and strengthened its role in the story of the Israelite nation.
With the passing of Hezekiah and the prophet Isaiah, Josiah (640-609 B.C.) and the prophet Jeremiah took up the battle against the idolatrous cults which had spread in the Kingdom under Manasseh. The pagan altars were destroyed and human sacrifice was prohibited while the Temple of Jerusalem became the center of national worship. Pilgrims filled the city on the three great holy days: Pesach, or Passover, in memory of the exodus from Egypt; or Sukkoth, or Tabernacles, recalling their stay in provisional shelters during the crossing of the desert; Shavuoth, the Feast of Weeks, which commemorates the giving of the Tables of the Law on Mount Sinai.

FROM THE BABYLONIAN CAPTIVITY TO THE EDICT OF CYRUS

A s Assyrian power waned, Egypt and Babylonia came into prominence. Judah found itself between the two Empires, and despite its strenuous defense, in 587 B.C. Jerusalem was conquered by Nebuchadnezzar. The city was sacked, the Temple destroyed, and tens of thousands of citizens were deported to Babylon. This was the beginning of the Babylonian Captivity where Jerusalem remained alive in the hearts of the exiles. In Psalm 137 is the heart-rending evidence: "By the rivers of Babylon,

The city and its mighty walls and towers, in the Holyland Hotel scale model.

there we sat down, yeah, we wept, when we remembered Zion. We hanged our harps upon the willows in the midst thereof. (...) How shall we sing the Lord's song in a strange land? If I forget thee, O Jerusalem, let my right hand forget her cunning, let my tongue cleave to the roof of my mouth; if I prefer not Jerusalem above my chief joy (...)".
In 539 B.C. Babylon fell to Cyrus, the founder of a great new empire, that of the Persians. He issued an edict, which acknowledged the right of the Jews to worship as they pleased and to return to their homeland. Thus began the return to Jerusalem.

REBUILDING THE TEMPLE AND THE PHASE OF HELLENIZATION

U nder the guidance of Zerubbabel the first caravan of Israelites left Mesopotamia for Jerusalem, but once there, they had to wait years before beginning the reconstruction of the Temple. At long last, in 520 B.C., still under Zerubbabel, work

was begun, to end in 515 B.C. when the Temple was consecrated.

This Temple was built on the foundations of the first one but it was simpler, subdued. All traces of the Ark had been lost, and the empty Holy of Holies was no longer separated from the holy place by a door but by a curtain, a veil of colored linen.

The prophets Ezra and Nehemiah helped reorganize the religious life of Israel. The Temple Mount, the Hill of Ophel, the City of David and the Pool of Shiloah were included in the new circle of walls, built by Nehemiah around 445 B.C., which surrounded the city and provided access through eight gates.

There is little existing evidence of the history of Jerusalem in the centuries that followed, until the Persian Empire fell to Alexander the Great, of Macedon, in 332 B.C. On his death, in 323, the Empire was divided among his generals, the Diadochi; Egypt fell to Ptolemy and Syria and

Babylonia to Seleucus. Later however Ptolemy prevailed and transferred a large number of Judaean prisoners to Alexandria where they formed a colony which was gradually Hellenized.

Under the Ptolemaic dynasty, Jerusalem and Judah prospered, while the Temple continued to be the beacon from which the light of the Jewish faith shone. Under Ptolemy II, the Old Testament was translated into Greek in the version known as the Septuagint, called so after the 70 wise men brought for the task to Alexandria from Jerusalem.

SELEUCID DOMINATION AND THE MACCABEAN UPRISING

*T*he benevolent Ptolemaic domination of Jerusalem continued for a brief time under the dynasty of the Seleucids who, with Antiochus III, had

A bird's eye view of the scale model; in the foreground Herod's palace with the Citadel on the left; in the background the Temple and the Antonia Fortress.

the Temple was reconsecrated and the feast of Hannukkah commemorates this event. In 142 B.C. one of the brothers, Simon Maccabeus, declared the independence of Judea and began the Hasmonean dynasty (from the name of the great grandfather of Mattathias, according to Flavius Josephus).

ROMAN OCCUPATION

The Hasmonean reign witnessed the formation of various religious sects, which were often at odds with each other. The Pharisees (that is the "separated") consisted mostly of scribes who strictly observed the Law. In the synagogues they spread the knowledge and devotion to the Holy Scriptures among the middle and lower classes and encouraged the faithful to scrupulously observe them. They also believed in the resurrection of the just who would then enjoy the benefits of the Kingdom of God. Their name alludes to the fact that they kept themselves separate from the pagans (the Gentiles), from unfaithful Jews and anything that might be considered impure. The Sadducees, whose name probably derives from Saduq, a priest with hereditary rights in the times of David and Solomon, were a priestly oligarchy from which the High Priest was chosen and which exercised control over the life of the Temple in Jerusalem. They considered themselves the true interpreters of the Laws of Moses and did not accept the doctrine of resurrection. Static in the field of theology and politically conservative, they displayed a practical opportunism and kept up relations with the Greek and Roman worlds. Their influence on the people was limited, bound as they were to the world of the Temple. Lastly there were the Essenes who led an ascetic life as they awaited the coming of the Messiah and his kingdom.
These sects were to play an important role under Roman domination, complying with it, or where possible, rejecting it.
In 63 B.C. when the Roman legions under Pompey invaded Palestine the people of Israel once again lost their freedom. Palestine was what the Romans called this land, an altered version of the name Philistia which at the time indicated the coastal strip along the Mediterranean occupied by the Philistines. When Hyrcanus II was deposed, in 37 B.C., the Roman Senate named Herod, later known as Herod the Great, King of Judea.
Suspicious and sanguinary, he always governed with the support of the Romans, who placed their troops at his disposal. He was not a loved leader; the Pharisees were always hostile and never forgave him his foreign origins (his father was an Idumean), the havoc wreaked by the Hasmonean dynasty, his friendship with the Romans, and the fact that he set an eagle, symbol of Rome, in the Temple.

succeeded in defeating the Ptolemaic forces (198 B.C.). However with Antiochus Epiphanes, who came to the throne in 175, things changed: he wanted all his subjects to live in Greek fashion, and Jerusalem, despite the fact that part of the population was in favor, rebelled. Riots broke out giving the sovereign a pretext for entering, plundering and desecrating the Temple. Pagan rites were celebrated in the Holy Court, pigs were sacrificed on the altar and the Scrolls of the Law were destroyed. The observance of Hebrew precepts, as well as the non-observance of pagan rites, were punished by death. The orthodox Jews, the Hassidim (the pious), resisted by following their faith in secret but persecution reigned until passive resistence gave way to guerrilla warfare. The leaders were Mattathias and his five sons; this was the glorious revolt known as the Maccabean Uprising (167-166 B.C.), which led to the liberation from Seleucid rule. Three years after its desecration

JERUSALEM IN THE TIME OF HEROD

*H*erod, ambitious, with a taste for oriental luxury, but not indifferent to art, enriched the city of Jerusalem with splendid buildings such as the royal palace, the Antonia Fortress and his sumptuous enlargement of the Temple. His palace, near what is now the Jaffa Gate, included the three towers of Fasel, Ippicus and Mariame on the north, and looked like a fortified citadel, enclosed on the north and west by the walls of the first circle and on the south and east by others that were specially built.

The Antonia Fortress, so called in honor of Mark Antony through whom Herod had obtained the throne, was actually an enlargement of the Hasmonean fortress which stood at the northwest corner of the Temple. Herod transformed it into a massive castle set on a high base complete with four corner towers. During the Jewish holidays, the southeast tower housed the Roman garrison, ready to intervene in case of disorder. Inside there were courtyards, baths, and halls which made it seem a luxurious palace.

Herod also endowed the city with other splendid buildings such as the theater, the hippodrome, and the Psephinus tower.

HEROD'S TEMPLE

*I*n the eighteenth year of his reign, Herod began work on enlarging the Temple and in order to win over the Jews, he had a thousand priests learn the craft of masonry so that the sacred areas of the Temple would not be defiled by impure hands.

The plan itself was not changed but the height of the Temple was increased and the area extended; various courtyards were added to the main building, set on an enormous esplanade built for the purpose and reached through eight gates. The two gates on the south side, called the Triple and the Double from the number of openings, led into the Royal Stoa or Portico comprising 164 columns set in four rows; on the east was the Portico of Solomon which contained schools, banks and shops. Between these two porticoes was the Court of the Gentiles, where pagans also had access; inside was a balustrade with thirteen openings which marked the area of the sanctuary and was strictly out of bounds for non-Jews, under penalty of death. From there a staircase led to the level on which the actual Temple stood. The sacred enclosure included the Women's Courtyard from which another staircase led to the Courtyard of the Israelites (for men only) and the Priests' Courtyard. Between these two was the sacrificial altar. Access to the sanctuary was from the Priests' Courtyard; a square forecourt, 50 meters per side, led through a wooden door covered with gold to the Holy Place, at the center of which was the Altar of Perfumes, on one side the seven-branched gold candlestick and on the other the Table of Loaves offered to God. A double veil of linen separated the Holy Place from the devir: this room was in the shape of a cube 20 meters per side and the only thing inside was a stone which indicated the place where the Holy Ark once stood. The

façade of the Temple was covered in gold.

Although from the architectural viewpoint Herod's Temple is the third to be built, it is considered the second by the Jews, for the one built by Zerubbabel had not been completely destroyed.

JUDEA, A ROMAN POSSESSION

*W*hen Herod died in 4 B.C., the Kingdom was divided among four of his many children: Judea and Samaria went to Archelaos who was deposed by the Romans (A.D. 6) and procurators were thereafter sent from Rome to act as administrators. There was a brief period between A.D. 41 and 44 when Agrippa became King of Judea. Grandson of Herod and his wife Mariame, he was of Hasmonean descent and therefore acceptable to the people; moreover, since he had been raised at the Court of Rome, he was a childhood friend of the Emperor Caligula and therefore also acceptable to the Romans. During his brief reign Agrippa built another circle of walls, known as the third, to surround the new suburb of Bethesda that lay to the northwest of the city.

Roman domination however became ever harder to bear. Under the procurator Gessius Florus, massacres became more frequent and the desire for liberation increased among the Jews who, in growing numbers, joined the ranks of the Zealots, an extremist sect which advocated armed battle against the Romans. The revolt turned into a real war in A.D. 66, which continued until it was brought to an end by Titus, son of the Emperor Vespasian, in the 70s. Jerusalem made a desperate attempt at defense, but to no avail. The closing acts of this battle took place outside the walls of the Temple; Titus then razed the fortress to the ground and attempted to breach the Temple compound. Finally he set fire to the doors: the metal covering melted and the wood burned through. When the fire died down, the soldiers fought the Jews at close quarters until they arrived at the Court of the Gentiles and then, one court after the other, they broke through the last defenses and set fire to the sanctuary. The population was massacred and the city, with the exception of the three towers of Herod's palace, razed to the ground. Those who were left were enslaved and forced to fight wild beasts in the victory celebrations organized at Caesarea. Other survivors were taken prisoner and led to Rome where they took part in the triumphal procession of Titus. The Zealot chief Simon Bar Giora was publicly executed in the Roman forum.

JESUS AND THE BEGINNINGS OF CHRISTIANITY

*J*esus was born in Bethlehem (probably in 4 B.C.) and spent his childhood in Nazareth. At that time many Jews were awaiting the coming of a Messiah (the annointed of the Lord) who was to make the Israelite nation great once more, freeing it from the Roman yoke. When Jesus began preaching, he was seen as the awaited Messiah and many followed him as he moved through the country. He often spoke of the coming Kingdom of God and his ideas conflicted with those of the principal religious sects of the time, the Sadducees and the Pharisees. Both feared his innovative ideas with respect to the Torah (the Law) and his proclamation of the new kingdom that was to come, aware that there would inevitably be violent clashes with the occupying Romans. It must also be kept in mind that false Messiahs had already appeared and that the title of "Son of God" was considered blasphemous.

Their fears increased when, on the feast of Pesach, Jesus entered Jerusalem. The Romans, fearing uprisings, were on the alert - as was always the case on the occasion of the feasts which brought thousands of pilgrims to Jerusalem - the priests were alarmed by the way in which Jesus arrived at the city gates, for he came riding on a mule, fulfilling the words of the prophet Zechariah who announced the coming of a king: "Rejoice greatly, O daughter of Zion; shout, O daughter of Jerusalem: behold, thy King cometh unto thee: he is just, and having salvation; lowly, and riding upon an ass, and upon a colt the foal of an ass. And I will cut off the chariot from Ephraim, and the horse from Jerusalem, and the battle bow shall be cut off: and he shall speak peace unto the heathen: and his dominion shall be from sea even to sea, and from the river even to the ends of the earth" (Zechariah. 9, 9-10). If the Romans were to interpret the arrival of Jesus as did the Jews who went to meet him, waving palm branches and singing the verse of a psalm - "Hossanna! ("oh Eternal, hail!") Blessed is he who comes in the name of the Eternal!" - seeing in him the prophesied king, their repression of the Jews would surely become harsher. These fears led the priests and the other members of the Sanhedrim, mostly Sadducees, to oppose Jesus. Taken on the Mount of Olives, east of the valley of Kidron, he was first brought to the palace of the High Priest Caiaphas, which appears to have been on the hill southwest of the Temple, beyond the Tyropoeon, and then to the Praetorium to be tried by the procurator Pontius Pilate. Although the Antonia Fortress is traditionally identified with the Praetorium, it was more likely the Palace of Herod. The death of Jesus, in a period of continuous tensions and frequent executions, did not cause much of a sensation, and his disciples, who kept the memory of Christ alive and spread his message, passed almost unobserved in Jerusalem. Indeed, Christianity developed outside of Judea.

AELIA CAPITOLINA

*I*n A.D. 130 the Emperor Hadrian went to Jerusalem and, aware that Hebrew nationalism was still alive, issued a series of edicts forbidding circumcision and the observance of the Sabbath. This unleashed the last and most desperate insurrection, headed by Simon Bar-Kokhba, who succeeded in governing Jerusalem for about three years, and continued his struggle around Jerusalem up to A.D. 135. He died on the 9th day of the Hebrew month of Av, a date that had also marked the destruction of the Temple of Solomon as well as that of Herod.

Hadrian destroyed what remained of Jerusalem, then built a new city in its place, Aelia Capitolina, laid out like a Roman encampment: crossed by the cardo and the decumanus, with the Forum at their intersection and gates at the ends. A temple to Jupiter was raised on the area of the Temple.

The Temple had already been destroyed by Titus and never rebuilt, but the Emperor Hadrian deemed it necessary to wipe out the sites venerated by the other faction, that of the Christians, and buried the Calvary and the Sepulchre under tons of earth; then on the earth fill he built the temple dedicated to the Capitoline Triad (Jupiter, Juno, Minerva). This custom of building the temples of the various religions on the same holy sites of the faith one hoped to replace was however what preserved their memory. The precise spot of Christ's Passion was marked by the presence of the pagan temple, and could no longer be mistaken for any other place.

In their attempt to erase all that recalled Israel, Judah and the Jews, the Romans also changed the name of the region: by then it was a province of Syria and was to be called, as noted earlier, Palestine.

A world away from the splendor of Jerusalem, Aelia Capitolina, closed to the Jews (they approached it under penalty of death) was nothing more than one of many small provincial cities.

Judah no longer existed as a nation and the Jews became a minority in their land.

CONSTANTINE AND THE HOLY SEPULCHRE

*I*n A.D. 324 Constantine was the head of the Byzantine Empire and therefore also ruled over Jerusalem. Converted to Christianity, he convoked the Council of Nicaea (325) which his mother, Helena, also attended, and it was here that she met Makarios, bishop of Aelia Capitolina. He told Helena about the deplorable conditions in which the holy places of Christianity found themselves, and Constantine's mother decided to go and see for herself.

Once in the city, Helena identified the site of the Crucifixion and of the entombment of Christ, as well as others locations which had witnessed the final episodes of the life of Jesus. The discovery of the remains of the true Cross was also ascribed to Helena.

Constantine then decided to construct buildings worthy of housing the holy places. In A.D. 326 excavation began to unearth and isolate the rock in which the tomb of Christ had been dug and the rock of Golgotha, where the Crucifixion had taken place. Afterwards the Anastasis, a circular building with its entrance on the east surmounted by a great dome supported by columns, was built to enclose the tomb of Jesus: the imperial architects Zenobius and Eustazius of Constantinople were entrusted with the construction. East of the Anastasis a portico was built which embraces the rock of Calvary on the southeast corner. A great basilica with five aisles, in line with the central entrance of the Anastasis, was built on the site where the Cross was found; this building too, called Martyrion, had the entrance facing east on an open atrium from which a few steps led onto the cardo maximus. Two corridors which flanked the north and south aisles of the building also led from this atrium to the Anastasis *without having to pass inside the basilica.*

Constantine was not the only one to build in Jerusalem: in the centuries that followed many wealthy Christians funded the building of churches, monasteries and hospices for pilgrims. The city, still out of bounds for the Jews except for a single day in the year - the 9th of Av - when they could go and pray at the Western Wall on the plaza (which from then on has been known as the Wailing Wall), was completely Christian.

During the 5th century the Empress Euodocia lifted this ban and had a church built to the north of the present Damascus Gate, in memory of the martyrdom of Saint Stephen, the first Christian martyr. She also had a sumptuous palace built and enlarged the city walls which now once more enclosed Mount Zion and Mount Ophel.

In the 6th century, under the Emperor Justinian, the Church of Santa Maria Nuova was built near the Wailing Wall.

PERSIAN OCCUPATION

*K*hosrow II, the Persian Emperor, laid siege to Jerusalem at the beginning of the 7th century, in A.D. 614. But this time the Jews sided with the besieger, as they wanted to free themselves of Byzantine domination. When the Emperor Heracleus ordered all Jews in his Empire to adopt the Christian faith, many enlisted in the Persian army. Great numbers of Christians were killed and the churches destroyed including the Martyrion and the Anastasis, but Jerusalem was not restored to the Jews.*

Modestus, a priest, was entrusted to administer the City. His name is remembered for the reconstruction of several churches and the Holy Sepulchre. He followed the early plans but the building never regained its original splendor.

In 629 Heracleus defeated Khosrow and the region again passed under Byzantine control; there were again massacres of the Jews and once more the survivors were expelled from the City.

ISLAM ARRIVES IN JERUSALEM: THE OMAYYADS

*M*ohammed, prophet of the new religion that saw the light in Arabia, died in 632; his successors, called caliphs, took over the task of consolidating Muslim authority in the Arabian peninsula and of spreading it into the neighboring countries. The second Caliph, Omar, declared war on Byzantium and Persia and in 638 laid siege to Jerusalem. Thanks to peace negotiations, the City surrendered without bloodshed and the Jews, despite the opposition of the Christian Patriarch Sophronius, were allowed to return to Jerusalem again. For four centuries they were able to profess their religion undisturbed and live in peace.*

Under Muslim occupation the holy character of the city remained intact: in fact, in one of his visions Mohammed had been transported to the Temple of Jerusalem on his legendary horse and from there he had risen to heaven, in the presence of God. This event, narrated in a sura (chapter) of the Koran, makes Jerusalem the third holy city of Islam, after the Mecca, where Mohammed was born, and Medina where he found refuge and died. For the Muslims Jerusalem was to be El-Kuds, The Holy, or El-Kuds esh-Sharifa, that is the Noble Saint.*

On the flat space of the Temple, called by the Arabs Haram esh-Sharif (or Noble Enclosure), Omar then built a wooden mosque, but his name is bound particularly to the imposing building raised in A.D. 687 by Abd al-Malik, caliph of the Omayyad dynasty.

Designed by Byzantine architects to enclose the rock from which the prophet had risen to heaven, the Mosque of Omar or Dome of the Rock has remained practically the same, despite earthquakes and restorations, up to our time and its dome continues to glow in the Jerusalem sky.

It is, however, to Abd al-Malik's son, the Caliph Al-Walid, that the construction of the Mosque of Al-Aksa is attributed. With its silvery dome, it stands on the south of the esplanade, but very little remains of the original building. Damaged by earthquakes, it was restored more than once. The most substantial work took place under the Fatimid Caliph Al-Zahir with the realization of the dome and the seven doors (1034).

During the Omayyad period, the Jews were once more allowed to live in the City and they settled in the quarters southwest of the Temple. They were permitted to come and pray at the Wailing Wall and, according to some sources, to build a synagogue in the quarter. Gradually, as their number increased, they also occupied the northern zone towards what is now the Damascus Gate.

Jerusalem was never the seat of government under the Omayyads: the capital of the Arab empire was Damascus, except for a brief period in which it was Ramla, the only city the Arabs built in the region.

UNDER THE ABBASIDS, THE FATIMIDS, THE SELJUK TURKS

*I*n 750 the Caliph Abu al-Abbas, known as Al-Saffah, ousted the Omayyads and the Abbasid dynasty began governing from Baghdad until 877. These sovereigns left a free hand to the mercenary Turks who gradually assumed increasingly important offices until one of their chiefs, Ahmed ibn-Tulun, ousted the Governor of Egypt. He no longer submitted to the authority of Baghdad and conquered Syria and Palestine, which of course included Jerusalem, and the region thus became an Egyptian province.*

The next Arab dynasty, that of the Fatimids, from Tunisia, took power in Egypt in 969. The Caliph Al-Aziz extended his rule to Jerusalem and allowed both Christians and Jews to continue in their religious faiths. But his successor Al-Hakim (996-1021), known as "the Mad Caliph", ordered the destruction of synagogues and churches in the empire. The same fate befell the Holy Sepulchre (1009) which was rebuilt in 1048 by the Byzantine Emperor Constantine Monomachus, who however failed to follow the plan of the Constantinian building.

The Muslim geographer Muqaddasi, born in Jerusalem in A.D. 946, left us a description of the City before it was struck by the wrath of Al-Hakim: the picture he gives is that of a large prosperous city, with many buildings and holy sites; a prosperous trading center with the streets filled with foreigners throughout the year. And it is true that under Arab domination Jerusalem witnessed a flourishing of trade and studies.

Half a century of tranquility followed the death of Al-Hakim, but it was brought to an end by the invasion of the Seljuk Turks, recently converted to Islam. Originally from the Islamic far east, near China, they ousted the Fatimids and in 1077 sacked Jerusalem, persecuting Jews and Christians during the twenty-five years of their reign. Their hostility to the Christians led to the First Crusade.

THE CRUSADER KINGDOMS

On July 15, 1099, after a siege of five weeks, and despite the strenuous defence put up by the inhabitants, Jerusalem was conquered by the forces of Godfrey of Bouillon and the Crusader banner was hoisted over the two mosques of the esplanade. Jews and Muslims were chased through the streets of the City and massacred with unheard of ferocity: several hundred Jews were burned alive in the synagogues which had been set on fire. The Mosque of Omar was then transformed into a church and that of Al-Aksa became the seat of the Knights of the Temple (Templars).

When Godfrey, who had assumed the title of Guardian of the Holy Sepulchre, died (1100), the throne of Jerusalem was offered to his brother Baldwin, and thus again became a capital. Once more and for 87 years, which was how long the Crusades lasted, the City was out of bounds to all those who did not belong to the conquering religion: neither Jews nor Muslims could live in Jerusalem.

Churches, monasteries and religious hospices flourished in the City in those years. But what mattered most of all was furnishing the Basilica of the Holy Sepulchre with new dignity. A church was erected in the court in front of the Anastasis, the chapels built by Constantine Monomachus were connected via an ambulatory set behind the apse of the Crusader church, and the Calvary was renovated with a vaulted roof.

In the northeastern quarter, where Baldwin had settled the Syrian Christians who had been called in to boost the scanty population that remained in the City, (then called Syrian quarter, today it is the Muslim quarter), the Crusaders built various churches including that of Saint Anne. Religious buildings also rose in the Armenian Quarter, which still bears that name (situated in the southwest part), in that of the patriarch, the present Christian quarter (to the northwest), and in what is now the Jewish Quarter, (to the southeast).

The perimeter of the City was basically no different from that of Roman times, and there were four main gates which opened in the city walls.

In 1187 Jerusalem again fell to the Muslims led by Saladin, son of the Governor of Damascus, who founded the Ayyubid dynasty. He reconsecrated to Islam the two mosques on the esplanade desecrated by the Crusaders and, unlike the preceding conquerors, was tolerant both towards the Christians and the Jews, who were once more allowed to live in the city.

The Christian West called the Third Crusade at this point to reconquer what had been lost. Important centers were recaptured, but not Jerusalem. Richard the Lionheart signed an agreement with Saladin acknowledging the western coastal strip with Acre and Jaffa as Crusader areas.

When Saladin died the Empire was divided among his sons who lacked the greatness and abilities of their father. The Emperor Frederick II profited from the conflicts that arose between the two branches of the dynasty (Egyptian and Syrian), and after being called in by the Sultan of Egypt, Al-Kamil, he received the City of Jerusalem as a reward, with the exception of the esplanade with the two mosques.

In the following decade the Crusader Princes were often in disagreement and also intervened in the rivalry between Cairo and Damascus, so that once again in A.D. 1244 Jerusalem was conquered and sacked by the troops of the Sultan of Egypt, who were nomad Turks of central Asia.

THE MAMLUKS

The Ayyubid dynasty came to an end with the death of Ayyub (1249). For 267 years government was in the hands of the Mamluk Sultans, who were descendents of the slaves (which is what the word Mamluk means) of Turkish tongue, originally from the Caucasus and central Asia, who had enlisted in the army of the Caliph of Baghdad. Great patrons of the arts and great builders, they realized four Madrasahs in Jerusalem (mosques with annexed Koran schools) and embellished the Haram esh-Sharif with fountains, porticoes crowning the staircases around the Mosque of Omar (the mawazin), and various small chapels. They also transformed many churches, including that of Saint Anne, into mosques, but their attitude to other religions was tolerant. Although Christians and Jews were taxed and obliged to wear blue and yellow turbans respectively to distinguish them from the rest of the Muslim population, they lived relatively tranquil lives.

In the second half of the 13th century the Ramban Synagogue was erected in the city by Moshe ben-Nahman and the group of Spanish Jews he had led to Jerusalem. It served as the rallying point for the Jews who arrived later as a result of the expulsions decreed by the Sovereigns of Spain (1492) and Portugal (1496).

Gradually the Mamluks lost interest in Jerusalem, which was after all a provincial city. Worn out by natural calamities such as famines, epidemics and earthquakes, it started on the road to decline.

THE OTTOMANS AND SULEIMAN
THE MAGNIFICENT

In 1517, with little bloodshed, Jerusalem passed to the Ottoman Turks who had conquered Constantinople in 1453, bringing to an end the Byzantine empire. Works carried out by the Sultan Suleiman the Magnificent between 1520 and 1566 still characterize the City. He rebuilt the walls with an unquestionable artistic sense and his Damascus Gate is noted for its grace as much as for the solidity

The scale model of the Temple with the elegant colonnade around the esplanade.

of its structures. He also repaired the aqueducts which supplied the city with water, built public fountains and embellished the Dome of the Rock with the splendid facing of arabesque blue-ground tiles and elegant stained glass windows.

While Jews were persecuted in Europe, under Suleiman the Jewish and Christian communities continued to profess their faith freely.

However, a decade after Suleiman's death, corruption began to rear its head among the governing officials who were interested solely in acquiring wealth rather than in governing the City. Taxes and tolls were exacted from the religious communities and pilgrims, constituting practically the only source of income for the Turks. This did not stop Jews and Christians who wanted to visit the holy sites from coming to Jerusalem.

As time passed the situation gradually worsened, except for brief periods in which more honest officials were in charge of the government. While the Christians, burdened by all kinds of taxes and excise duties, managed to live thanks to the protection of the European powers, the Jews were more and more at the mercy of the whims, not only of the local authorities, but also of the individual Muslim citizens. Despite this, Jerusalem never stopped being a magnet for Jews who continued to arrive from Europe, swelling the local population.

In the second half of the 16th century - although the Christian pilgrims had already been following the Via Dolorosa or Street of Sorrows as early as the 13th and 14th centuries - fourteen stations of the Way of the Cross were established, not all corresponding to the present ones, in commemoration of the Passion of Christ.

Serious episodes of intolerance, in addition to the burdens mentioned above, marked the years of the Ottoman rule. In 1580 the Pasha took over the synagogue of the Spanish Jews which had become the most important in Jerusalem, and transformed it into a mosque, but thanks to corrupt officials and at the cost of enormous sacrifices another one was built. In 1720, the Synagogue built twenty years earlier by Yehuda Hahassid, who had arrived from Poland with a group of Ashkenazi Jews (as Jews from central and northeastern Europe are called, while those of western and southern Europe, the Middle East and northern Africa, are Sefardic) burned down. The perimetral walls remained standing and it was then called Synagogue Hurva, or "ruin". The Ashkenazi were driven out of Jerusalem and were prohibited from reentering.

During the 19th century there was a sharp rise in the number of Jews coming to Jerusalem. They were fleeing from the ghettos of Rome, Russia, Poland, and Turkey where they were the object of ridicule, humiliation and persecution. Around 1860 the more than 10,000 Jews living in Jerusalem were the greater part of the population. In 1860 the first quarter outside the city walls was built, thanks to an English Jewish benefactor originally from Livorno, Sir Moses Montefiore. Other quarters soon followed, including Me'a She'arim, Mahaneh Yehuda and Yemin Moshe.

In the wake of the Zionist movment founded by Theodor Herzl in the last quarter of the century, there was a considerable increase in the flow of immigrants. The pioneers, who bought land from the corrupt Ottoman administrators, began to reclaim swamps, farm the land and build villages.

THE FALL OF THE OTTOMAN EMPIRE AND THE BRITISH MANDATE

The Ottoman Empire, started dissolving in the course of the 19th century as a result of the nationalist uprisings of the Balkan peoples which had led to independence, was overwhelmed by World War I. Allied to the central powers, the great body of the Ottoman Empire was dismembered and vast

areas entered the sphere of influence of the victorious nations.

The final months of 1917 played a decisive role in the development of subsequent events. November 2nd, the date of what then came to be known as the Balfour Declaration, is an important date for Jews throughout the world who dreamed of living in a state of their own. Lord Balfour declared, on behalf of the British government, "His Majesty's Government view with favour the establishment in Palestine of a National Home for the Jewish People..." On December 9th Jerusalem handed itself over to the English General Allenby.

After the Balfour Declaration, at its meeting in 1922, the League of Nations approved the British Mandate over Jerusalem and Palestine which was to last until 1948.

There was a surge of immigration in these years from the countries of central and Eastern Europe, where the Fascist regimes were also coming to power. This increase in the Jewish population led to clashes with the Arabs, partially because the customs and political and social ideas of the newcomers were different from those of the Jews who had lived side by side with the Muslims for centuries.

In the meantime Jerusalem was taking shape as a capital: the Hebrew University was inaugurated in 1925 on Mount Scopus, in 1938 the Hadassah Medical Center was established and then the City became the seat of the National Council. The years of the British Mandate were not peaceful years for Jerusalem: violent disorder often broke out which resulted in an increasingly restrictive attitude towards the Jews on the part of the British. Anti-

Semitism intensified. The shiploads of Jews in flight from Europe were refused by the British who decided in 1939 to limit entrance into the country to 100,000 persons during the next five years, despite an awareness of Hitler's projects aimed at exterminating the entire Jewish nation.

AFTER WORLD WAR II - THE STATE OF ISRAEL

*I*ncredibly the restrictions established in 1939 were to be maintained until after the end of World War II, when tens of thousands of Jews who had managed to survive the Holocaust sought refuge in the land of their Fathers. This prompted the reaction of the Jewish armed organizations who blew up the King David Hotel in Jerusalem, the British administrative headquarters (July 1946). The following year the British relinquished their Mandate and in November the General Assembly of the United Nations voted in favor of a plan which provided for the partition of Palestine into an Arab state and a Jewish state, but which was however rejected by the Arab world.
On May 14, 1948 David Ben Gurion proclaimed the sovereign State of Israel, but the Arab countries attacked with the aim of "throwing the Jews back into the sea". Israel was the victor after seven months of war , but the Jewish quarter in Jerusalem remained in the hands of the Jordanian troops who had destroyed all existing synagogues and study centers.
The armistice set the borders along the line of the ceasefire which cut Jerusalem in two in a north-south direction passing near the Wailing Wall, on the west the new city and Mount Zion in Israeli hands, everything on the east in the hands of Jordan except for Mount Scopus. The agreement provided for free access for the Israelis to the University and the Hadassah Medical Center, as well as to the Wailing Wall for prayer, but actually nothing was ever permitted and Jerusalem remained divided.
Both Jordan and Israel began to develop their respective areas. The Jordanians were interested in the City primarily because, except for the Tomb of David and the Cenacle (Room of the Last Supper), all the holy sites of the three religions were in their hands, and were seen as an important source of income from pilgrimages and tourism. This was why they built a great deal outside the walls and improved their part of the Old City where the bazaars were to be found. The Israelis, on their part, had to deal with the waves of immigrants who wanted to settle in the City. They had to endow it with all the facilities required by a capital and receive all the officials who made it their headquarters. Development of the Israeli part was, therefore, greater and included the construction of factories and government buildings, as well as dwellings.
By 1966 the building for the Knesset, the Israeli Parliament, was also ready.

THE SIX DAY WAR AND THE REUNIFICATION OF JERUSALEM

*T*he morning of June 5, 1967 the sirens sounded in Jewish Jerusalem: war had broken out. The capacity for a pre-emptive strike to the combined attack of Egypt, Jordan and Syria was exceptional. In only six days not only was the enemy thrown back, but vast areas of those countries fell under control of the Israelis who had occupied the Sinai, the West Bank of the Jordan, the Gaza Strip and the Golan Heights. But above all, Jerusalem was reunited under the flag of the Star of David: on June 7th at 9:50 a.m. the Israeli troops arrived at the Wailing Wall.
After the official reunification, on June 27th, the inhabitants of each quarter gradually began to circulate throughout the City and succeeded in living together as no one had ever imagined.
The Yom Kippur War (1973), initiated by Egypt but also involving Syria, provided the premises for the Peace Treaty between Egypt and Israel (1977) although nothing basically changed on a military level. Other events have sorely tried the tenacity of the Israelis while trying to have their right to live in the Land of their Fathers acknowledged: the civil war in Lebanon, the attacks carried out by extremist groups and Islamic Fundamentalists and the Gulf War. Despite the bombs, the aggressions and the blood shed by both sides, the olive twig planted in the Agreements of Camp David has become a tree which has born unimagined fruits. On September 13, 1993 in Washington, in the White House gardens, Itzhak Rabin, Shimon Peres and Yasser Arafat shook hands before the American President Bill Clinton and millions and millions of spectators who were watching the historical event on their television screens. A year later Jordan too signed the Peace Treaty with Israel acknowledging its right, always denied by the Arabs, to exist as a state.
Three thousand years have passed since David unified the twelve tribes of Israel under his rule. Wars, persecutions, suffering, foreign domination attempted over and again to wipe out even the memory of these peoples. Now we can all look to the future with renewed faith and hope.
Disagreement still exists as to what has been, and what still is to be, done, but the most important step on the road to peace has been taken. With Israeli and Palestinian understanding and collaboration, two peoples who have demonstrated, each in their own way, a love of and attachment to the land on which they live, can, and surely will, know how to provide an example of civilization for the entire world.
Then Jerusalem will finally see the Hebrew meaning of its name translated into reality: CITY OF PEACE for all peoples.

Jerusalem as shown in the Madaba mosaic, the Cardo flanked by columns is clearly visible.

Gregorian calendar	Jewish calendar	Muslim calendar	LAND OF CANAAN	FOREIGN EVENTS
ca. 3000 B.C.	ca. 760		Early Bronze Age Development of Jericho Contacts with the Egyptians	**Egypt** - Kingdom of Upper Egypt and Kingdom of Lower Egypt. Unification of the two kingdoms under Narmer. Old Kingdom. III Dynasty: Zoser builds the stepped pyramid of Sakkara. IV Dynasty: building of the pyramids of Sneferu, Cheops, Chefren and Mycerinus

Mesopotamia - The Sumerians in the south of Mesopotamia. City- states. Building of the walls at Uruk. The temple takes on the shape of a ziggurat

Aegean - Beginning of the Early Minoan Period |
| ca. 2500 B.C. | ca. 1260 | | Middle Bronze Age Egyptian contacts with Byblos | **Egypt** - V Dynasty. Crisis of the supreme power. VI Dynasty. Fall of the unitarian state. Beginning of the First Intermediate Period

Mesopotamia - The Assyrians settle in northern Mesopotamia, in the zone of the upper Tigris. I Dynasty of Ur. I Dynasty of Lagash: the last Sumerian king, Lugalzaggisi, conquers Lagash, Ur, Uruk, Larsa, Kish and Nippur. His kingdom is replaced by the kingdom of Akkad with Sargon I who founds a centralized state. Foreign domination of the Gutians. III Dynasty of Ur. Restoration of the kingdom of Sumer and the kingdom of Akkad

Aegean - Development of the Early Minoan Period. Beginning of the Middle Minoan Period

Greece - Early Helladic Period |
| ca. 2000 B.C. | ca. 1760 | | **HEBREW TRIBES**

First migrations from Ur in Chaldea. Abraham is received in Shalem by the king Melchizedek | **Egypt** - Middle Kingdom. XI Dynasty: Mentuhotep II unifies Egypt with capital at Thebes. XII Dynasty: Amenemhet II and Sesostris III expand the Egyptian empire as far as Megiddo in Palestine and Ugarit on the Syrian coast. Second Intermediate Period: internal unrest favors invasion by the Hyksos (Hurrite peoples and Semitic races). Ahmose drives out the Hyksos and founds the New Kingdom

Mesopotamia - The Sumerian kingdom is invaded by the Semitic Canaanites. Formation of states at Isin, Larsa and Babylonia. End of the III Dynasty of Ur and growth of the Assyrian power which conquers the north Babylonian territory. Old Assyrian kingdom. The Hittites, an Indoeuropean race who live in Anatolia, invade the country. Subsequently Hammurabi becomes king of Babylonia. Code of Hammurabi and termination of the palace of Mari. Development of literature in Akkadian tongue: Epic of the Creation of the World and the Gilgamesh Epic

Aegean - First Palace Period in Crete (Knossos, Phaestos and Mallia) followed by the New Palace Period in Knossos (the Labyrinth), Phaestos and Hagia Triada. Foundation of the kingdom and thalassocracy (maritime supremacy)

Greece - End of the early Helladic Period and beginning of the Middle Helladic Period. Infiltrations of Indoeuropean tribes. Ionians and Aeolians (Achaeans) fuse with the local Mediterranean populations. Beginning of the Mycenaean Period |

Gregorian calendar	Jewish calendar	Muslim calendar	HEBREW TRIBES	FOREIGN EVENTS
ca. 1500 B.C.	ca. 2260		The children of Jacob in Egypt. Middle of the 13th century: Moses and the Exodus. Late 13th-early 12th century: Joshua. Conquest of Canaan. Period of the Judges. The Philistines settle along the southern coast of today's Israel	**Egypt** - XVIII Dynasty: great expansion of the Egyptian empire. In the 14th century: Amenophis III and Amenophis IV/Akhenaten. In the 13th century: Ramses II reconquers Syria (battle of Kadesh). Under Merneptah the exodus of the Jews from Egypt. Ramses III drives the Philistines from the Delta. Third Intermediate Period **Mesopotamia** - Babylonia is conquered by the Kassites, from Iran. Middle Assyrian empire: Tiglathpileser I consolidates the power of the kingdom **Aegean** - Crete is conquered by the Mycenaeans who assimilate the civilization. Destruction of the palace of Knossos **Greece** - Greatest expansion of Mycenae. Construction of beehive tombs and fortification of Mycenae, Tyre, Pylos, Athens. Lion Gate and Treasury of Atreus at Mycenae. Dorian migration takes place around 1150 **Asia Minor** - Troy is destroyed around 1250
ca. 1020 B.C.	ca. 2740		Saul struggles against the Ammonites. Saul is proclaimed king	**Mesopotamia** - Assyrian empire
ca. 1000 B.C.	ca. 2760		David reunites the north of the country (Israel) with the south (Judah) and is anointed king at Hebron. He conquers Jerusalem and makes it the capital of the unified Kingdom of Israel	
ca. 971 B.C.	ca. 2789		Solomon, David's successor, builds the Temple of Jerusalem (First Temple)	Hiram is king of Tyre
ca 930 B.C.	ca. 2830		Country is divided into the kingdom of Judah to the south under Rehoboam, with Jerusalem as its capital, and of Israel to the north under Jeroboam with Shechem as its capital (later Tirzah and Penuel and lastly Samaria). The Pharaoh Sheshonq I invades the Kingdom of Judah	
			KINGDOM OF JUDAH **KINGDOM OF ISRAEL**	
ca. 885--874 B.C.	ca. 2875--2886		The king Omri founds Samaria	**Assyria** - Neo-Assyrian empire **Italy** - Gradual take over of the territories between the Tiber and the Arno by the Etruscans, probably originating in Asia Minor
ca. 870--848 B.C.	ca. 2890--2912		Jehoshaphat	**Assyria** - Tiglathpileser III founds the Assyrian empire. His successor Shalmaneser V lays siege to Samaria **Greece** - Beginning of the Olympic Games

TIME CHART 3

Gregorian calendar	Jewish calendar	Muslim calendar	KINGDOM OF JUDAH	KINGDOM OF ISRAEL	FOREIGN EVENTS
ca. 722 B.C.	ca. 3038		Hezekiah. The prophet Isaiah	Hoshea. Samaria is conquered by Sargon II, successor of Shalmaneser V. End of the Kingdom of Israel	**Assyria** - Reign of Sargon II **Italy**- Founding of Greek colonies in the southern part of the peninsula and in Sicily. Founding of Rome in 750

KINGDOM OF JUDAH

Gregorian calendar	Jewish calendar	Muslim calendar	KINGDOM OF JUDAH	KINGDOM OF ISRAEL	FOREIGN EVENTS
705-681 B.C.	3055-3079		In 701 Sennacherib lays siege to Jerusalem, but the city miraculously is the only one which succeeds in resisting the Assyrian forces		**Assyria** - Sargon II is succeeded by his son Sennacherib who destroys Babylon and subjugates the Kingdom of Judah. Assyrian Empire achieves its greatest expansion
698-644 B.C.	3062-3116		Manasseh, son of Hezekiah, is vassal of Assyria. Idolatry spreads		
640-609 B.C.	3120-3151		Reign of Josiah, great grandson of Hezekiah. Beginning of Jeremiah's prophesizing		**Mesopotamia** - Rise of Babylon: all the Assyrian cities are conquered and destroyed
587 B.C.	3173 (9 of Av)		Nebuchadnezzar II lays siege to Jerusalem. Destruction of the Temple. Beginning of the Babylonian Captivity		**Mesopotamia** - Reconstruction of Babylon under Nebuchadnezzar II: Ishtar Gate, Tower of Babel, Processional Avenue

JUDEA

Gregorian calendar	Jewish calendar	Muslim calendar	KINGDOM OF JUDAH	KINGDOM OF ISRAEL	FOREIGN EVENTS
538 B.C.	3221		Judea is under Persian dominion. Thanks to the Edict of Cyrus the Great, the Jews are freed from bondage and allowed to return to their homeland		Cyrus the Great of Persia conquers Babylonia. The Persian Empire expands throughout the Orient, except for Egypt. Cyrus is succeeded by Cambyses (529-522) who also conquers Egypt. Under Darius I (521-486), First Persian War against the Greeks who under the leadership of Miltiades win the Battle of Marathon (490). Under Xerxes (485-465), Second Persian War against the Greeks: in 480 the sack of Athens; Greeks victorious in the naval battle of Salamina
515 B.C.	3244		The Temple rebuilt by Zerubbabel is consecrated		
445 B.C.	3316		Nehemiah rebuilds the walls of Jerusalem		**Persian Empire** - Artaxerxes (464-424). Darius II (423-405). Artaxerxes II (405-359). Alexander the Macedonian conquers the Persian Empire
332 B.C.	3429		Judea is under the dominion of Alexander the Great who arrives in Jerusalem		
323 B.C.	3438		Judea is under the dominion of Ptolemy I King of Egypt. Judean colonies in Egypt. Translation of the Old Testament into Greek (Septuagint version). Appearance of the Hassidim (the pious)		Death of Alexander and division of his empire. Ptolemy I King of Egypt. Ptolemy II Philadelphus King of Egypt. Hellenism. Wars between Carthage and Rome (264-202). Rome Mediterranean power
198 B.C.	3562		Judea passes under the Syrian dominion of the Seleucids. Antiochus II and Seleucus IV Philopator favor the Jews		**Syria** - Dynasty of the Seleucids: Antiochus III defeats the Ptolemaic armies. Seleucus IV Philopator

Gregorian calendar	Jewish calendar	Muslim calendar	JUDEA	FOREIGN EVENTS
167 B.C.	3593		Desecration of the Temple of Jerusalem by Antiochus IV Epiphanes Appearance of the Essenes	**Syria** - Antiochus IV Epiphanes (175-164)
167-164 B.C.	3593-3597		Maccabean Uprising. Purification of the Temple of Jerusalem	
142 B.C.	3618		Simon Maccabees declares independence of Judea. Beginning of the Hasmonean dynasty. Sadducees and Pharisees: their respective doctrines are at odds Orcanis I succeeds Simon Maccabees	**Syria** - Antiochus VII (141-129) is the last of the Seleucid kings
63 B.C.	3697		Pompey annexes the country to Rome. Orcanis II is deposed by the Romans and becomes high priest	Caesar rises to power in Rome
37 B.C.	3723		Herod the Great is elected by Rome to be King of the Jews. Monumental works in Jerusalem and reconstruction of the Temple	Augustus Roman Emperor (27 B.C. - A.D. 14)
Beginning of the Christian era	3753		Birth of Jesus. Beginning of the Christian era. Herod the Great dies. The kingdom is divided among his children: Judea and Samaria to Archelaos (later replaced by Roman procurators); Galilee to Herod Antipas; northeastern provinces to Philippus; region of Damascus to Lisanias	
A.D. 18 - 36	3778-3796		High priest Caiaphas. The Zealots begin their resistence to the Romans	Tiberius Roman Emperor (14-37)
A.D. 26 - 36	3786-3796		Pontius Pilate is governor of Judea. Christ is crucified in 33	Caligula Roman Emperor (37-41)
A.D. 41 - 44	3801-3804		Herod Agrippa is the last Hebrew king of the country. The third circle of walls is constructed in Jerusalem. When he dies the Roman procurators return. In 44 Saint Paul visits Jerusalem	Nero Roman Emperor (54-68)
A.D. 64 - 66	3824-3826		Gessius Florus procurator of Judea. The revolt of the Zealots begins: the Romans decimate the Jews	Rome burns in July 64
A.D. 70	3830 (9 of Av)		Titus, Vespasian's son, conquers Jerusalem and destroys the Temple. The Diaspora of the Jewish people begins	Vespasian Roman Emperor (69-79)
A.D. 130	3890		Hadrian in Jerusalem. Edicts banning circumcision and the observance of the Sabbath precept	Hadrian Roman Emperor (117-138)
A.D. 132 - 135	3892-3895		Bar Kokhba Insurrection. The Romans are driven from Jerusalem Hadrian retakes the city and razes it to the ground: in its place he builds the Roman Aelia Capitolina, out of bounds for the Jews The Romans give Judea the name of Palestine	
A.D. 324	4083		Judea is made part of the Empire of Byzantium	Constantine, Emperor of Byzantium; first Christian emperor, in 325 calls the Council of Nicaea

Gregorian calendar	Jewish calendar	Muslim calendar	JUDEA	FOREIGN EVENTS
A.D. 326	4085		Constantine in Jerusalem. Restores Christian holy sites. Holy Sepulchre. The city is completely Christianized. Jews are still banned, except for one day in the year	In 476, with the deposition of Romulus Augustulus, the end of the Roman Empire of the West
ca. A.D. 570	ca. 4329			Mohammed (Abul Kasim el-Mohammed) is born in Mecca, in Arabia. After 610 he begins to preach the monotheistic doctrine of Islam
A.D. 614	4373		The Emperor Heraclius imposes conversion to Christianity, and as a result the Jews help the Persians to conquer Jerusalem. Destruction of the Holy Sepulchre and various churches and the massacre of the inhabitants of the City	Heraclius Byzantine Emperor (basileus). Khosrow II Emperor of Persia
A.D. 622	4381	Beginning of the Muslim era		The Muslim calendar begins on July 16. The prophet Mohammed leaves Mecca (**Egira**) and takes refuge in Medina
A.D. 629	4389	8	Heraclius comes back to power: further massacres of the Jews who are once more expelled from the country	
A.D. 632	4392	11		The prophet Mohammed dies. He is succeeded by the Caliph Abu-Bekr and in 634 by the Caliph Omar Ibn al-Khattab
A.D. 638	4397	17	Omar conquers Jerusalem without shedding blood. The Jews are once again allowed to live in the City: Jerusalem (in Arabic El-Quds, meaning The Holy) is the third holiest city of Islam	Expansion of the Arabian empire in Syria, Persia and Egypt
A.D. 661	4420	41		Beginning of the Omayyad dynasty. The capital of the Arab Empire is Damascus
A.D. 687	4446	68	Abd al-Malik builds the Dome of the Rock or "Mosque of Omar" in Jerusalem. His son Al-Walid builds the mosque of Al-AksaAbd al-Malik builds the Dome of the Rock or Mosque of Omar in Jerusalem. His son Al-Walid builds the mosque of Al-Aksa	Expansion of the Arabian empire in northern Africa
A.D. 750	4510	133	Under Ahmed ibn-Tulun, Jerusalem and the country become an Egyptian province	End of the Omayyad dynasty. Beginning of the Abbasid dynasty. Capital: Baghdad
A.D. 969	4729	359	The Fatimid Al-Aziz extends his rule to Jerusalem. Christians and Jews are free to profess their own faiths	The Fatimids come to power in Egypt
996 - - 1021	4756 - - 4781	386 - - 412	Al-Hakim is caliph and destroys churches and synagogues. In 1009 the Holy Sepulchre is destroyed	In 1054 the break between the Church of the East and that of the West (Great Schism)
1077	4837	470	The Seljuk Turks sack Jerusalem. Jews and Christians are persecuted	

Gregorian calendar	Jewish calendar	Muslim calendar	JUDEA	FOREIGN EVENTS
1099	4859	492	The Crusaders under the command of Godfrey of Bouillon conquer Jerusalem. Jews and Muslims are slaughtered. The following year Jerusalem, capital of the Crusader Kingdom, is closed to Jews and Muslims	
1187	4947	583	Saladin conquers Jerusalem. Jews and Christians can live in the City	Salah ad-Din (Saladin) founds the Ayyubid dynasty
1229	4989	627	Al-Kamil, Sultan of Egypt, gives the city of Jerusalem to the Emperor Frederick II	
1244	5004	642	The troops of the Sultan of Egypt conquer Jerusalem, which is plundered and its inhabitants massacred	
1249	5009	647	The Mamluks in Jerusalem: religious tolerance	
1453	5213	857		Constantinople is besieged and falls into the hands of Mohammed II, Ottoman Emperor. End of the Roman Empire of the East. The city becomes the capital of the Ottoman Empire under the name Istanbul
1492	5252	897		Christopher Columbus discovers America. The Spanish sovereigns expel the Jews from the country
1516	5276	922	Jerusalem becomes part of the Ottoman Empire	
1520 - 1556	5280 - 5326	928 - 974	Suleiman the Magnificent is Sultan of Jerusalem. He builds the present walls of the city and the Damascus Gate. Other works beautify Jerusalem. Freedom of religion for Jews and Christians	Suleiman raises the Ottoman Empire to its greatest splendor
1914 - 1918	5674 - 5679	1332 - 1337		World War I
1917	5678	1336		Balfour Declaration
1918	5679	1337		End of the Ottoman Empire
1920	5681	1339	British Mandate in Palestine	
1939 - 1945	5699 - 5705	1358 - 1364		World War II
1948	5708	1367	David Ben Gurion proclaims the sovereign State of Israel	
1949	5710	1369	Jerusalem is officially proclaimed capital of the State of Israel	
1967	5727	1387	Unification of Jerusalem	

There is some deviation in dates due to differences among the calendars.
The **Gregorian Calendar** is a solar calendar, with 365 days divided into 12 months. An extra day is added every four years (29 February).
The **Jewish Calendar** is lunisolar. It is based on a lunar year (12 months of 29-30 days), but the month of Adar is repeated about every 3rd year to bring it into line with the solar calendar. The months do not match those of the Gregorian Calendar. The new year is always celebrated on the first day of the month of Tishri (which falls in September-October of the Gregorian Calendar). The Jewish Calendar is based on the Old Testament, and began in the year 3769 (before the Christian or Current Era) that is, the year of the Creation.
The **Muslim Calendar** is lunar. The year has 354 days; every thirty years there is a cycle of eleven years comprising 355 days so that gradually, every month falls in each season.

In the IV-V century the monk Dionysius Exiguus (Denis the Little) determined the date of Jesus' birth as 25 December of the year 754 *ab Urbe condita*, that is from the founding of Rome, and our current dating system went into effect the following year. Actually, there was an error in his calculations and Jesus' birth year should be moved to 747 or 748 *ab Urbe condita*. Therefore, to find the exact year Jesus was born, we must add 6 or 7 years to the current one. This table, however, is based on the commonly used calculations to indicate the years before and after the start of the Christian or Current Era.

THE CITY INSIDE THE WALLS

THE WALLS AND THE GATES

THE TOWER OF DAVID OR CITADEL

THE JEWISH QUARTER

THE CHRISTIAN QUARTER

THE MUSLIM QUARTER

THE ARMENIAN QUARTER

CITY MAP

Inside the Walls

1 Mount Moriah
2 Mosque of Omar
3 Al-Aqsa Mosque
4 Gate of the Chain
5 Golden Gate
6 Wailing Wall
7 Wilson's Arch
8 Robinson's Arch
9 Dung Gate
10 Hurvà Synagogue
11 Cardo
12 Ophel Archeological Garden
13 Lion's Gate
14 Church of St. Anne
15 Pool of Bethesda
16 Herod's Gate
17 Chapel of Ecce Homo
18 Church of Our Lady of the Passion
19 Red Mosque
20 Damascus Gate
21 Church of the Holy Sepulchre
22 Lutheran Church of the Redeemer
23 Muristan
24 Church of Terra Santa
25 Latin Patriarchate
26 Jaffa Gate
27 Citadel-David's Tower
28 Anglican Christ Church
29 Cathedral of St. James
30 Church of St. Mark
31 Armenian Patriarchate
32 Armenian Seminary
33 Zion Gate

Outside the Walls

34 Dormition Abbey
35 David's Tomb
36 Cenacle
37 Church of St. Peter in Gallicantu
38 Pool of Shiloah
39 Gihon Spring
40 Absalom's Pillar
41 Church of All Nations
42 Church of Dominus Flevit
43 Church of Saint Mary Magdalene
44 Aedicula of the Ascension
45 Russian Tower
46 Tomb of the Virgin
47 Rockefeller Museum
48 Garden Tomb
49 St. Stephen's Basilica
50 Tombs of the Kings
51 Anglican Cathedral of St. George
52 Italian Hospital
53 Russian Cathedral
54 City Hall
55 Herod's Tombs
56 Y.M.C.A.
57 King David Hotel
58 Yemin Moshe
59 Great Synagogue
60 Monastery of the Cross
61 Israel Museum
62 Knesset
63 Menorah

SULEIMAN

16

BAB HUTTA

AQAB, SHADAD

15
14

DOLOROSA

13

EL WAD (HAGAI)

DIYE

SHELET

MISGAV

LADA

BATEI MAHASE

1

2

5

4

7

6

8

3

12

9

MA'ALEH HA-SHALOM

MALHIZEDEK

37

YERUSHALAIM

38

39

DERECH HA-SHILO'AH

DERECH YERIHO

DERECH HA-OFEL

DERECH HA-OFEL

DERECH HA-SHILO'AH

46

41

40

43

44

42

45

47

63

54

56

62

57

59

61

60

25

THE WALLS AND THE GATES

One of Jerusalem's outstanding features is the splendid circle of grey stone walls that runs for about four kilometers, rising to a height of twenty meters. The walls were built by Suleiman the Magnificent between 1536 and 1542, when the city was under Turkish domination; there are seven famous gates. The most beautiful is the **Damascus Gate** at the entrance to the old road leading north. Recent excavations have brought to light the remains of the ancient Roman entrance. **Herod's Gate** leads to the Muslim Quarter.

The **Lion's Gate** opens towards the Mount of Olives; Christians call it St. Stephen's Gate because they believe that the saint was stoned to death on that spot, while the Muslims call it Bâb Sitti Maryam, that is, the Virgin Mary's Gate, believing it to be the site of her birthplace. The **Golden Gate** or Gate of Mercy is quite unusual, as it is divided by two arches that the Muslims closed. Tradition maintains that Jesus passed through here on his way to the Temple, and that the Byzantines built the gate over foundations that date back to Solomon's era. The **Dung Gate**, which gets its name from the fact that in biblical times there was a rubbish dump just outside the walls, leads directly to the area of the Wailing Wall.

The **Zion Gate**, which leads to the Jewish and Armenian quarters was built by the sultan Suleiman the Magnificent in 1541. The Arabs call it Bâb ed-Daoud which means "of David" because it faces Mount Zion, traditionally believed to be the burial place of David. And finally, the **Jaffa Gate**, named after the old port, opens onto the main route leading west. Its traffic and strategic position make it the most important junction in the old city. Known as Bâb el-Khalili in Arabic, it has two openings: the smaller one is the original, while the other was created in 1898 to make room for the procession of the Kaiser Wilhelm II. The **New Gate** was opened in 1889.

A gate from the Ayyubid period (XIII cent. A.D.) has been reopened west of the Dung Gate to provide pedestrian access to the Wailing Wall. Excavations nearby have brought to light some portions of the "Cardo Valensis" one of the city's main thoroughfares during the Byzantine period.

Two details of the splendid walls built by Suleiman the Magnificent.

The Ophel Archeological Garden at the foot of the southern wall of the Temple esplanade.

THE TOWER OF DAVID - THE CITADEL

The **Citadel** of Jerusalem, as it appears today, is a wall, reinforced by five large towers. It occupies the area where Herod's three towers once stood. He had them built around 24 B.C., and named them after his brother Fasel, his friend Ippicus and his wife, Mariame. They were so magnificent that when the Roman legions destroyed Jerusalem in 70 A.D., the Emperor Titus left them standing to show future generations their beauty.

The towers, however, did not survive the Emperor Hadrian, who ordered them torn down in 135 A.D., and left only the enormous bulk of the foundations.
It seems that the name **Tower of David** dates from the Middle Ages, when Christian pilgrims, awed by the imposing ruins, attributed them to the works of the biblical king. Partial restorations were made during the Arab conquest and during the Crusades when it was the

The Jaffa Gate, the Golden Gate and the Dung Gate which leads directly to the Wailing Wall.

The Citadel seen from above.

The monumental entrance and the inside of the Citadel.

*Two views of the excavations inside the Citadel
with the arch dating from the Mamluk period.*

residence of the Latin king. Then, following the
destruction wreaked by the later Muslim conquests, work
was done under the Mamluks and Ottomans when
Suleiman restored the Citadel and built the monumental
entrance which still stands today. The minaret was added
in 1635.

Remains of Hasmonean-period buildings provide
evidence that the city had again expanded westward
during that era (the first westward expansion took place
under Hezekiah in the VIII century B.C.).

Inside the Citadel, with its bastions surrounded by a
moat, there are three itineraries that can be followed:
through the archeological excavations, along the path of
the watch with its towers - offering an incredible view of
the city - , or via the museums. Rooms inside the towers
host the **Museum of the History of Jerusalem**. Maps,
scale models and impressive audio-visual presentations
illustrate the city's history from the Canaanite period to
our day. In one room there is a scale model of the entire
city of Jerusalem.

Herod's palace once stood south of the City, where
today's police headquarters are located.

The arch from the Mamluk period, the bastions with the minaret built in 1635.

The majestic tower and the minaret.

The scale model of the city as it was during the period of the First Temple.

*The Citadel during the
sound and light show.*

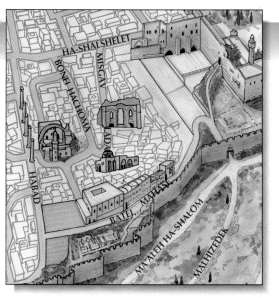

THE JEWISH QUARTER

The Jewish Quarter is located where the High City stood during the time of Herod. The Jews abandoned the area under Hadrian's reign, and it was only at the end of the crusades that rabbis and students of the various Jewish schools returned. It was occupied by the Jordanians during the 1948 War of Independence, and was razed to the ground during the Six Day War. Subsequently, large scale and systematic archeological excavations were undertaken, and brought to light the **Burned House**. The house had belonged to the Bar Katros, a family of temple priests, and had been burned during the destruction of 70 A.D.; it is open to the public and there are interesting artifacts on display. The quarter still bears traces of nearly every historical period, such as the Israelite Tower, the Broad Wall that was part of the walls dating from the period of the First Temple, the Herodian Quarter and the Cardo Maximus. The **Broad Wall**, discovered during the excavations begun after the 1967 war is seven meters wide, and was part of the fortifications built by king Hezekiah (701 B.C.). In the **Herodian Quarter**, remains of six elegant dwellings dating from 37 B.C. to 70 A.D. have been discovered. The lower stories are rich in mosaics and frescoes (that do not portray any human or animal figures, in accordance with the dictates of the Second Commandment) and include the ritual baths (mikvah) and cisterns. Particularly luxurious is the residence known as "the Mansion". These were the homes of the aristocracy during the period of the Second Temple.

A section of the Cardo, unearthed and restored.

CARDO

A few meters beneath the level of the existing road is the **Cardo Maximus**, the route that led from the Damascus Gate to the old Zion Gate which was located a little farther from the Zion Gate we see today. The road dates from the period of the Aelia Capitolina, yet its current features are from the Byzantine era when major restorations and building work were done.

The Cardo was a broad, colonnaded street, flanked by porticoes and shops. The part we can see today, with its columns and Corinthian capitals is about half as wide as the original. Farther down, below the modern buildings is the area that was the market during the crusader era. Today it hosts a unique shopping center. Along the ancient road with its ogival arches, are modern shops, where archeological evidence of various periods are intelligently highlighted and identified.

A glimpse of the Jewish Quarter and an enclosed section of the Cardo, lined with stores in a unique shopping center.

A lovely view of the Cardo from above: capitals with Corinthian columns, the minaret of the Sidi Umar mosque and the Hurvà Synagogue.

THE RAMBAN AND HURVÀ SYNAGOGUES

These two synagogues are located right near the open portion of the Cardo, next to the minaret of the Sidi Umar Mosque. **Ramban** is another acronym of the name of Rabbi Moshe ben Nahman, a great Talmudic scholar who arrived from Spain around 1267. The synagogue, divided into two naves by columns which probably belonged to the Cardo, is the oldest in Jerusalem along with the Karaite synagogue. It was closed by the Turkish government during the sixteenth century, then destroyed in 1948, and partially rebuilt in 1967 when it once again became a house of worship.

The **Hurvà** synagogue (the word means "ruin") is located right behind the Ramban, and can be easily recognized by the big arch that was part of the dome. Built in the eighteenth century by Polish Jews, followers of the famous Rabbi Yehuda ha-Hassid, it was destroyed several times, most recently in 1948 when the Arab League razed it to the ground.

Aside from restorations on the great arch and the inner courtyard, the synagogue has never been rebuilt, to show future generations how much devastation the district suffered.

Part of the Jewish Quarter and the Ramban Synagogue with the Hurvà Arch.

Two views of the Hurvà synagogue, only one of the four original arches has been rebuilt; below: the inner courtyard.

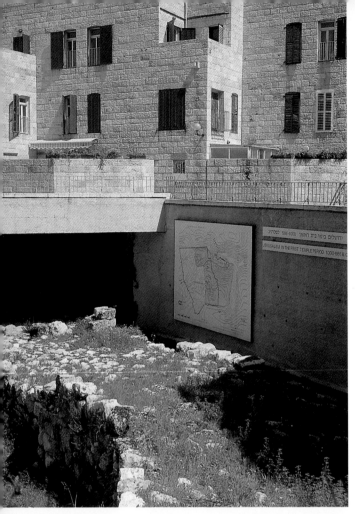

THE TIFERET ISRAEL SYNAGOGUE AND THE FOUR SEFARDIC SYNAGOGUES

Just a short distance from the Hurvà square are the remains of the **Tiferet Israel Synagogue** (that is, "glory of Israel"). Before it was destroyed in 1948, its outlines were clearly visible above the city's roofs. All that remains today are three, richly carved portals. Nearby, are also the ruins of the IX century **Karaite Synagogue**; the Karaites broke away from traditional Judaism in the VIII century A.D.

The heart of the Jewish quarter is located south of Hurvà square. It comprises the **Four Sefardic Synagogues,** a center of worship for the Jews who arrived here after being expelled from Spain in 1492. The complex was severely damaged in 1948: both the structure itself and the furnishings, nearly all of which disappeared. After the restoration work done in 1967, the synagogues were refurbished with arks (the cabinets in which the Torah scrolls are kept) that were brought over from Italy. They came from old synagogues of destroyed Jewish communities. So, for example, we can admire a finely decorated XVI century ark from Ancona in the Istanbul Synagogue, where Jews of Turkish origin would come to pray.

East of the Jewish Quarter is the large square that reaches to the foot of the Wailing Wall.

Restorations in the Jewish Quarter have preserved the archeological finds. Left, part of the archeological finds. Below, the three portals of the Tiferet Israel Synagogue.

The Jewish Quarter, with the Wailing Wall, the Temple Esplanade and the Mosque of Omar (on the following pages).

THE WAILING WALL

This is the symbol of the Jewish faith, for Jews from the world over: the **ha-Kotel ha-Ma'aravi** is a fragment of the western wall that was built to support the Temple Esplanade. It stands 15 meters high and was renamed the "Wailing Wall" because of the Jews' long exile. The Romans prohibited them from returning to their city, and the Byzantines only allowed them to go once a year, to pray on the anniversary of the destruction of the Temple (9th day of Av).

Between 1948 and 1967 the Wall was in the Jordanian sector of Jerusalem, so once again, Jews were denied access. It became the symbol of the reconquest of the city, and of the reunification of the enitre Jewish State. Therefore, when on 7 June 1967, the first Israeli troops reached the Wall, it marked a key event and an unforgettable date in the history of the Jewish people. Whether it is the 9th of Av when hundreds of Jews gather at the Wall (men separate from women in the orthodox tradtion), or late at night when just a few silent figures stand before the ancient, gigantic square-cut stones, nothing interrupts this silent, continuing dialogue. There are many traditions linked to the Wall: one of them is to write prayers and wishes on a bit of paper and slip it into the cracks between the stones.

The square in front of the Western Wall is a constant goal of the faithful who come here to pray. However, all Jews are forbidden from actually setting foot on the esplanade where the Temple stood. Since it is impossible to know its exact location, someone could accidentally step on the Holy of Holies where only the high priest was permitted to go.

Among the many Jewish group, the religious **Ashkenazi** (from Central-Eastern Europe) are easily recognizable. They wear shiny black coats, black trousers, black hats sometimes with fur-trimmed brims, long beards and side-locks. Others, from North Africa or Middle Eastern countries wear embroidered caps similar to those used by Muslims; others pray covering their heads and shoulders

Destruction and reconstruction have marked the history and appearance of Jerusalem over the centuries, so it is difficult to imagine the Temple Compound the way it must have looked.
Here is a rendering of Herod's Temple and the buildings on the Esplanade the way they would look today.

with prayer shawls ("talleth") with fringes at the four corners. All males, however, no matter what age, cover their heads.

The most orthodox among the Ashkenazi (from Ashkenaz in Germany) speak Yiddish, a Medieval Jewish-German dialect that has since become a literary language. These people use Hebrew, considered the holy language, only for study and prayer. The most radical of these do not recognize the State of Israel and reject its laws. They believe that only the advent of the Messiah will give the Jews sovereignty over Jerusalem and the Holy Land. The women of this community dress very modestly, and married women cover their heads with hats, wigs or scarves.

Sefardic Jews are those who originally came from Spain (from the Hebrew "Sefarad" meaning Spain) and the Mediterranean region. Their language was Ladino, a Judeo-Spanish dialect, and as far as ritual goes, they differ considerably from the Ashkenazi Jews.

Today the square serves as a synagogue, so religious observances may be held there, such as the Feast of the Tabernacles (Succoth) in the autumn. Prayers are said holding a citron ("etrog") in the left hand, and a palm tree branch bound up together with myrtle and willow in the right; there is a specific way of entwining the branches. Then both the citron and the branches (called "lulav") are waved in the four cardinal directions and up and down as a sign of joy.

Private ceremonies such as the Bar Mitzvah, that is, a boy's coming of age are also celebrated at the Wall. When a boy reaches the age of 13 he is considered an adult, and therefore responsible for his own spiritual life, and under obligation to observe fasts and other rituals. The boy puts on phylacteries ("tefillin"), small leather boxes containing parchment strips with verses from the scriptures, and dons the prayer shawl ("talleth") for the first time. After the blessings are recited, the boy is called to read a portion of the Torah before the congregation. The Sefer Torah, that is the Law, contains the first five books of the Old Testament; it is written by hand on a parchment scroll which is kept in a decorated cylindrical container. If the ceremony is held on the Sabbath, the phylacteries are not used.

The area in front of the Wailing Wall is an outdoor synagogue: Ashkenazi Jews at prayer, and Sefardic boys celebrating their Bar Mitzvah.

On the following pages, the Temple esplanade seen from two different angles.

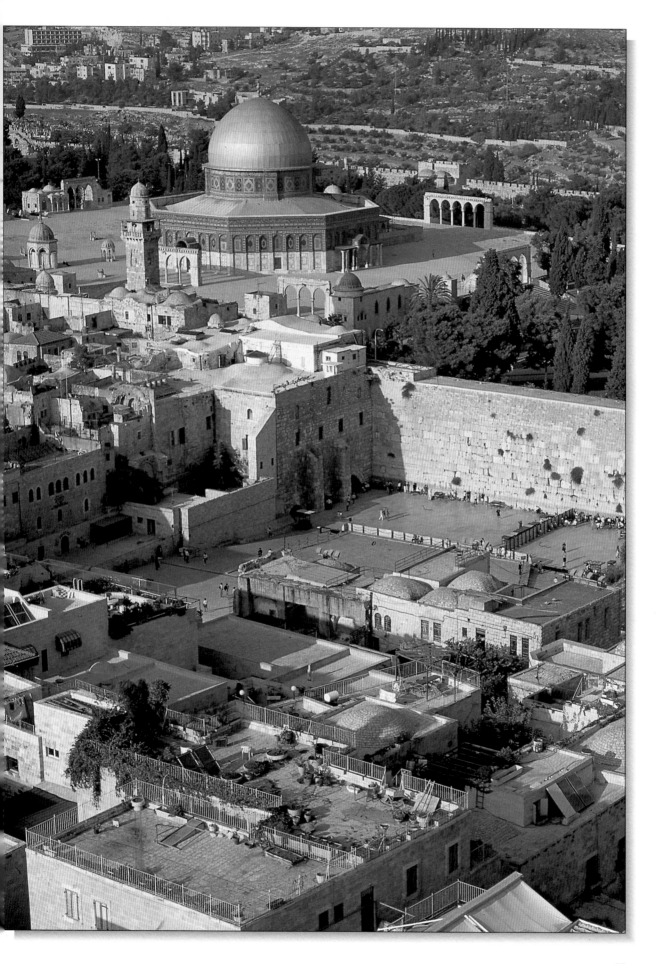

49

*Wilson's Arch, and above,
the remains of Robinson's Arch.*

Wilson's Arch. To the left of the Wailing Wall stands the arch named after Charles Wilson, the English archeologist who discovered it in 1865. Beneath the Medieval structure is the original arch dating from Herod's era. It supported the bridge which, during the period of the Second Temple, joined the High City with what is now the Haram esh-Sherif. Further excavations below the existing pavement level have revealed nineteen rows of squared stone blocks.

Robinson's Arch. The remains of this arch are at the southwest corner. The arch supported a staircase leading to the Royal Portico of the outside Temple enclosures on the side where the Al-Aqsa Mosque now stands. The four niches in the base of the structure have been identified as money changers' shops (offerings to the Temple had to be made in the local currency). The stone, protected by glass, engraved with a passage from Isaiah probably dates back to the period of the emperor Julian the Apostate.

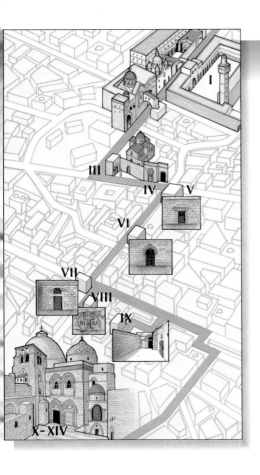

THE CHRISTIAN QUARTER

The Christian Quarter takes up the western part of the old city.
The Via Dolorosa follows Jesus' steps from his prison in the Antonia Fortress to the Calvary where He was crucified and buried. Most of the Way of the Cross winds through the Muslim Quarter and ends inside the Basilica of the Holy Sepulchre in the Christian Quarter. Other Christian holy places, linked to Jesus' life and miracles, like the Bethesda pool are located in the Muslim zone. Therefore, a "Christian" itinerary of Jerusalem must begin at the Lion's Gate, in the eastern side of the wall built by Suleiman the Magnificent: the house of Saint Anne and Saint Joachim stood nearby.

An impressive view of the Lithostratos inside the Convent of the Soeurs de Sion. Below, the dome and belltower of the Church of the Holy Sepulchre.

The Lion's Gate. This gate gets is name from the relief carvings of two pairs of lions that flank the ogive. Christians, however, call it St. Stephen's gate because tradition holds that it is where the saint was stoned to death. The Muslims, on the other hand, call it the Gate of the Virgin Mary (Bâb Sitti Maryam) because it is believed that the house where Mary was born stood nearby.

The Church of St. Anne. Immediately beyond and to the right of the Lion's Gate stands the Church of St. Anne on the traditional site of the home of Anne and Joachim, the parents of the Virgin Mary.

The building, one of the best preserved in the entire city was constructed in 1142 during the crusader period by order of Arda, wife of the King of Jerusalem, over the site of a previous VI century church. Fifty years later, however, Saladin had transformed it into a school for Koran studies (madrasah). In 1865 the Turkish sultan gave it and the surrounding land to the French Government and since 1878 it has been in the hands of the Catholic "White Fathers". Although it has undergone many restorations, this austerely beautiful church is a jewel of crusader art. The interior is divided into three naves, and a short flight of steps leads down to the Byzantine crypt which, according to tradition, is the birthplace of the Virgin Mary. Excavations alongside of the church have brought to light the remains of the Pool of Bethesda where Jesus healed the cripple.

The Lion's Gate gets its name from these bas-relief carvings.

The exterior, interior and crypt of the Church of St. Anne, a jewel of crusader art.

The Pool of Bethesda. The pool is located on the plateau of the same name, north of the Temple Mount. It was originally a water reservoir for the Temple itself. Since it was located near the ancient Sheep's gate, it was also called after the Greek word for sheep "probatike". It is here that John the Evangelist set the episode of the healing of the cripple. The structure, as brought to light by excavations was already described by St. John: two trapezoid-shaped basins with perimetral passages (the "porches" mentioned in the Gospel), joined by another central passage. Hadrian had a temple to Aesculapius, the God of Medicine built on the site. In the V century it was replaced by a Byzantine basilica dedicated to the Virgin Mary. The basilica was destroyed by the Persians in 614 and rebuilt by the crusaders, and the remains of this last building can be seen above the excavations.

There are several structures covering the area of the Antonia Fortress: an inscription on the door of a Greek-Orthodox building near the Convent the Soeurs de Sion indicates the **Prison of Christ**. The underground rooms are said to have been the prison where Jesus was held, however, there is no real proof that these grottoes had been used for that purpose.

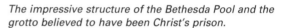

The impressive structure of the Bethesda Pool and the grotto believed to have been Christ's prison.

THE VIA DOLOROSA

Although the custom of retracing Jesus' steps to Golgotha began in the early centuries of Christianity, it was in the XVI century that the term Via Dolorosa (or Way of the Cross) came into use to indicate the approximate route Jesus followed bearing the burden of the Cross from the Antonia Fortress to the Calvary. The Fortress, Herod's residence, and also described as the seat of the Praetorium where Jesus was brought before Pilate, was destroyed along with the Temple in 70 A.D by the Emperor Titus. Only bits of the original floor and the entrance to one of the four corner towers remain.

The First Station (Jesus is condemned to death). The first station is located in the courtyard of the el-Omary Madrasah (school of Islamic studies) founded in the fourteenth century over the site of the Antonia Fortress. Every Friday, which is the Muslim holy day, it is the starting point for the procession, led by Franciscan monks, that ends at the Holy Sepulchre.

Every Friday pilgrims follow the Via Dolorosa, commemorating Christ's Passion.

A detail of the Via Dolorosa.

The exterior and inside of the Chapel of the Flagellation.

The Second Station (Jesus is made to bear his cross). This event is commemorated on the outside wall of the Chapel of the Condemnation which, like the Church of the Flagellation, is located in the courtyard of the Franciscan Monastery of the Flagellation on the right hand side of the Via Dolorosa, opposite the el-Omariyya Madrasah.

The window above the altar in the **Chapel of the Flagellation** portrays Jesus' suffering, while the mosaic on the dome depicts a large crown of thorns.

The **Chapel of the Condemnation** still has some of the stones of the Lithostratos, much of which can be seen in the nearby Soeurs de Sion Convent. The stained glass on the dome shows angels carrying the instruments of Christ's passion, Pilate washing his hands, and Jesus taking the cross.

Going along the Via Dolorosa we come to the **Ecce Homo Arch**. Actually, this is the central part of the triple arch that Hadrian built in 135 A.D. to mark the entrance to Aelia Capitolina, the Roman city built over the ruins of Jerusalem. The southern arch, towards the Temple area is partially preserved inside an Arab building, while the northern arch can beseen in the choir of the church of the Soeurs de Sion. Above the part spanning the street is an Arab home. The current name dates from the crusades and refers to Pilate's words, "Behold the man."

Both the **Convent of the Soeurs de Sion** and the **Chapel of Ecce Homo** rise over the site of the Antonia Fortress. From the back of the chapel we can see the remains of the fortified entrance to one of the fortress towers. Inside the convent, a flight of steps leads down to the **Lithostrotos** which, in the Gospels, is described as being opposite the Praetorium. It was here that Jesus was tried and whipped. This is substantiated by the fact that in addition to the little channels that served to drain off rainwater and carry it to the cistern below, the floor is marked for some of the games Roman soldiers used to play. One of these can be identified by the letter "B", the "game of the King", or "Basileus", in Greek.

The Ecce Homo Arch; the Lithostrotos and the "Basileus" game engraved on an ancient paving stone. Opposite, the Chapel of the Condemnation, and an interior view.

The cistern, or **Struthion Pool**, located beneath the Convent of the Soeurs de Sion supplied water to the troops garrisoned in the Antonia Fortress.

The Struthion Pool; below, the Convent of the Soeurs de Sion, the Virgin Mary's birthplace according to the Greek Orthodox congregation which oversees the place; right, an Arab man riding a donkey through the streets.

The Third Station (Jesus falls the first time). On the site where Jesus fell for the first time under the weight of the Cross there now stands a chapel built by Polish cavalrymen. The chapel is the seat of the Armenian Catholic Patriarchate, whose **Church of Our Lady of the Passion** presages the next station. In earlier days, a Byzantine chapel and a crusader church stood on this site.

The Fourth Station (Jesus meets his mother). This meeting is recalled by a small Armenian oratory. The Polish sculptor Zieliensky carved the bas-relief in the fine lunette over the door.

The Fifth Station (Simon of Cyrene is made to bear the cross). An inscription on the architrave of the door to a Franciscan chapel recalls the episode of Simon of Cyrene being made to carry the cross. The story is confirmed in the Gospels of Matthew, Mark and Luke.

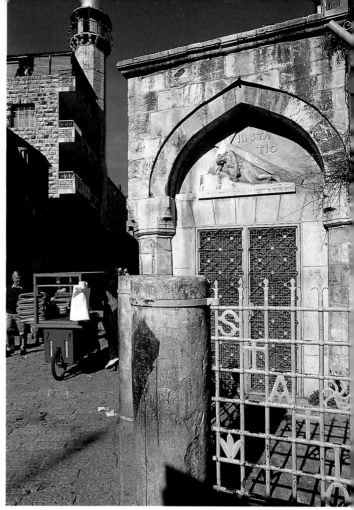

The chapels of the 3rd, 4th and 5th Stations of the Cross.

The 6th and 7th Stations along the Via Dolorosa, the cross marking the 8th Station; opposite, the interior of the Coptic Monastery of St. Anthony, the 9th station is marked on the outside.

The Sixth Station (Veronica wipes Jesus' face). The place where Veronica wiped Jesus' face is marked on the door of the Melchite chapel. The image of his face remained on the cloth.

The Seventh Station (Jesus falls the second time). Inside the Franciscan chapel that commemorates Jesus' second fall, there is a column from the Cardo. The chapel stands at the intersection that leads into the Christian Quarter of Jerusalem.

The Eighth Station (The women of Jerusalem weep over Jesus). A small, time-blackened cross is carved into the wall of a Greek-Orthodox monastery. It is here that Jesus said "Daughters of Jerusalem, weep not for me, but weep for yourselves and for your children..." (Luke, 23: 28).

The Ninth Station (Jesus falls the third time). A column next to the entrance of the **Coptic Monastery of St. Anthony** indicates the places where Jesus fell the third time; it is in a high position, behind the apse of the Church of the Holy Sepulchre.
The last five Stations are inside the basilica.

The Church of the Holy Sepulchre as seen by the XIX century English artist, David Roberts and opposite, the way it looks today.

THE HOLY SEPULCHRE

This is the most sacred Christian place in Jerusalem and the entire world. It is filled with history, tradition and faith arousing profound emotions in all visitors.

During Jesus' time it was outside the city gates and was probably higher than it is today because, being the site of public executions, it had to be readily visible from afar so that all could take heed. The place called Golgotha from the Aramaic word for skull, got its name from the fact that it was indeed skull-shaped, and from the legend maintaining that it is where Adam's skull was buried. The emperor Hadrian chose the site to build the capitol and a temple dedicated to the gods Jupiter, Juno and Minerva, as well as a small temple to Venus right on the Calvary, making it necessary to fill the cavities in the rock and level the ground. This, in turn, saved the underlying tombs from destruction.

When Helena, mother of the Emperor Constantine, learned from the Bishop Macarius in 325 that Golgotha and Jesus' tomb were probably located beneath the capitoline temple, she immediately ordered excavations that yielded positive results.

Constantine appointed the imperial architects Zenobius and Eustachius to create a true monument. The tomb was isolated by a large, round structure, the Anàstasis (Resurrection), while a cross topped by a ciborium was raised on the Calvary. On the eastern side of the Rotunda rose the basilica with five naves and the crypt of the Discovery of the Cross.

The first Church of the Holy Sepulchre was begun in 326, completed in 335 and destroyed by the Persians in 614. Fifteen years later the abbot Modestus had it restored.

It was destroyed again around 1009 by the caliph al-Hakim Bi-Amr Allah and restored by the Byzantine emperor Constantine Monomachus in 1084. When the Crusaders conquered Jerusalem on 15 July 1099 they did not consider the building worthy of housing Christendom's most holy places, so they began modifying and embellishing it. The new church was dedicated in 1149 and remained basically unchanged until 1808 when a major fire destroyed much of it. The Greek monks obtained permission to rebuild it, but their work significantly changed the original plan.

The Romanesque façade of the Holy Sepulchre dates from about the mid-twelfth century and hence the Crusades. Two overlapping rows of ogival arched lintels with classic fluted, leaf-motif friezes rest on columns with elegantly carved capitals.

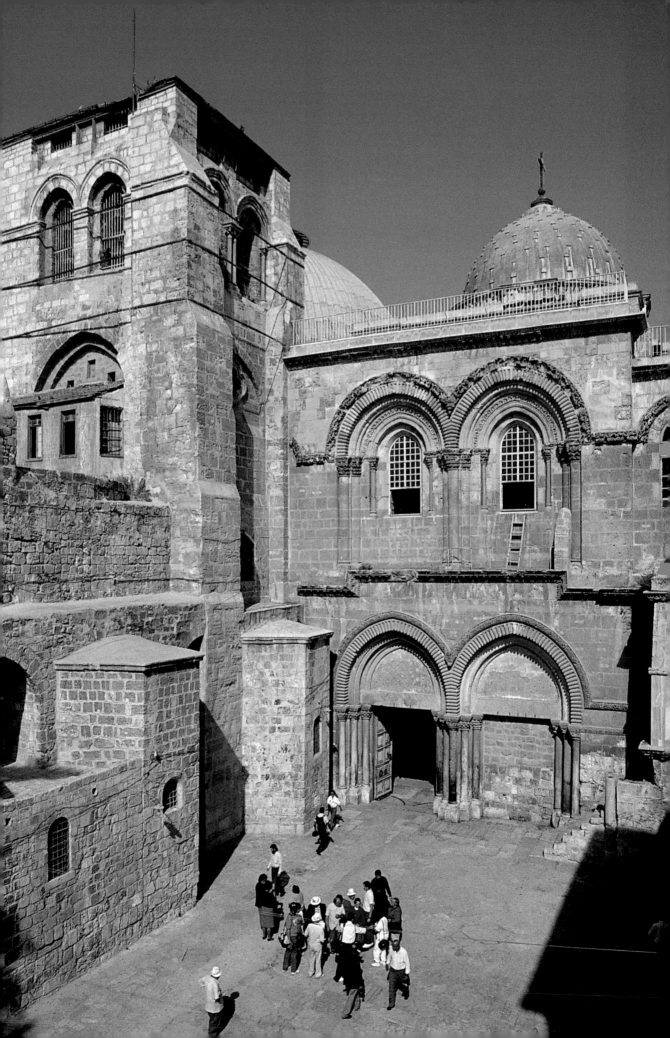

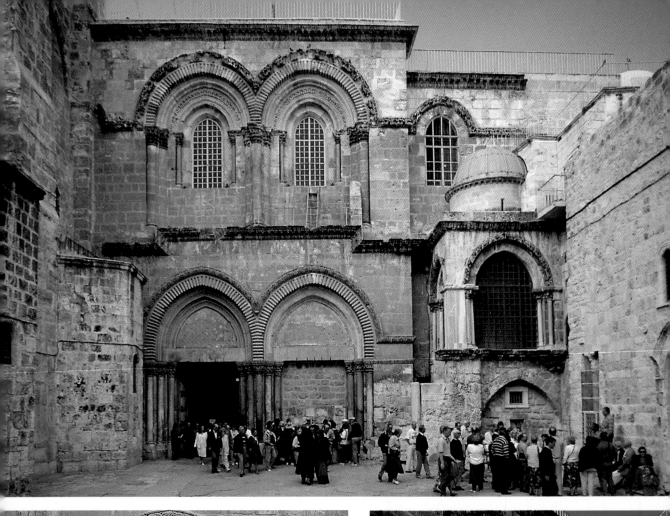

The courtyard outside the church, the door,
and the Frankish Chapel.

Worship outside the Armenian Chapel of St. John.

Currently the Holy Sepulchre is controlled by six
Christian groups: the Roman Catholic, Greek Orthodox
and Armenian churches oversee larger portions than the
Coptic, Syrian and Abyssinian congregations.
The church overlooks a paved courtyard, on the right side
are the **Greek Monastery of Saint Abraham** standing
over the western part of the Forum of Aelia Capitolina,
the **Armenian Chapel of St. John** and the **Coptic
Chapel of St. Michael**. On the left side we can see the
the apses of the three Greek chapels of **St. James**, **St.
John** and **the Forty Holy Martyrs**. The impressive bell
tower, that dates from the Crusades, rises above the last
of these three chapels, and it still bears the signs of when
the top collapsed in 1545.
The stairs to the right of the façade lead to the elegant
Medieval Frankish chapel which once led directly to
the Calvary. Beneath it is the **Chapel of St. Mary of
Egypt**.
The basilica has two identical ogival portals, but the one
on the right was bricked over during Saladin's era.
An ancient privilege has given custody of the surviving
door to two Muslim families: one keeps the key, and the

THE HOLY SEPULCHRE

1- Entrance hall
2- Muslims guards
3- Stone of the Unction
4- Chapel of Adam
5- Altar of the Nails of the Cross
6- Altar of Stabat Mater

7- Altar of the Crucifixion
8- Catholicon
9- Place of Mourning
10- Rotunda
11- Sepulchre of Christ
12- Coptic Chapel
13- Jacobite Chapel
14- Tomb of Joseph of Arimathea
15- Altar of Mary Magdalene

16- Franciscan Church
17- Arches of the Virgin Mary
18- Holy Prison
19- Chapel of Longinus
20- Chapel of the Division
   of the Holy Robes
21- Chapel of Saint Helena
22- Chapel of Derision
23- Latin Choir

The interior of the Holy Sepulchre in two drawings by David Roberts.

The Stone of Unction; following pages, Calvary, and the Chapel of the Crucifixion, separated by the small altar of the Stabat Mater.

other has the right to open it. Opening the door is a ceremony itself. In the morning the keeper of the key comes to the door, while the sacristans of the three main religious congregations of the church wait inside. A sacristan passes a ladder through a small window in the door. The keeper of the key takes the ladder and gives the key to the man who has the right to open the door who then climbs up to reach the lock and perform his task. The ladder is then passed back through the window, the door is unbolted on the inside, and finally opened. The solemn opening ceremony requires the contemporaneous presence of the three sacristans (Franciscan, Greek and Armenian) who perform the same tasks simultaneously, however the Franciscan must always be in the middle. The procedure is reversed to close the door. The only change in this ritual takes place between Holy Thursday and Good Friday when the key is taken by the Custodian of the Holy Land. On the morning of Good Friday, at the foot of the ladder, it is he who gives the key to the man who opens the door.

The Stone of Unction. Upon entering the church we see this slab of polished pink stone. Flanked by candles, with eight lamps hanging above it, it is the **XIII Station** (Jesus is taken down from the cross). The stone sets on the site of the former Oratory of the Unction which was taken down during the many architectural changes made to the building. According to tradition, Jesus' body was placed here when it was removed from the cross and anointed with myrrh and aloe.

The Calvary. A steep flight of steps on the right leads to the site of Jesus' execution. Now the place is occupied by the **Chapel of the Crucifixion** and the **Calvary**, which are separated by the Altar of the Stabat Mater honoring Our Lady of Sorrows. The first chapel, belonging to the Roman Catholic Church, commemorates the **X Station** (Jesus is stripped of his garments), and the **XI Station** (Jesus is nailed to the cross). The mosaic behind the Altar of the Nails depicts the Crucifixion. In the second chapel, which belongs to the Greek Orthodox church is the **XII Station** (Jesus dies on the cross). It is embellished by life-sized icons portraying Christ, the Virgin Mary and St. John. Beneath the image of Christ Crucified is a rock with a silver ring indicating the spot where the cross was raised.

Christ's Tomb. Inside the aedicula of the Holy Sepulchre is the **XIV Station** (Jesus is placed in the sepulchre) of the Way of the Cross.

The aedicula is situated in the center of the Anàstasis, and it is the result of centuries of changes made to an ancient Jewish tomb. The entrance leads into a larger room known as the **Church of the Archangel.** A fragment of rock marks the exact spot where the angel is supposed to have sat as he told the women about the resurrection.

The actual tomb chamber, a candle-lit arcosolium, is small and awe-inspiring. It is here that Christ completed his earthly mission before his glorious Resurrection in accordance with the prophecies.

On the preceding pages, the icon of the Virgin Mary in the Chapel of the Crucifixion, the Chapel. Three pictures of the Aedicula of the Holy Sepulchre.

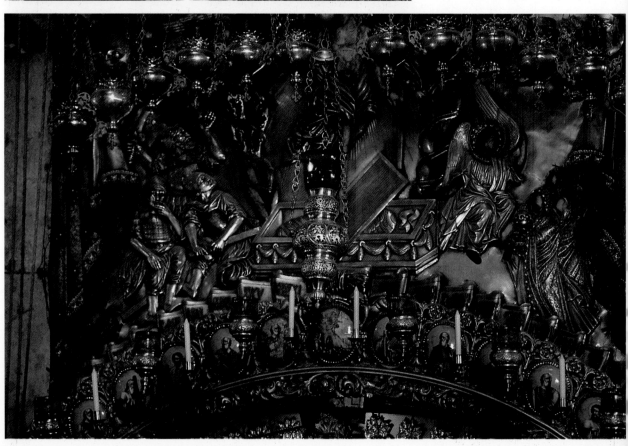

A marble slab on the right covers the original rock of the tomb that was located in the garden of Joseph of Arimathea. Above the tomb are many silver lamps belonging to the Catholic, Greek, Armenian and Coptic congregations. Above the stone are icons depicting the Greek, Latin and Armenian versions of the Resurrection.

The Church of the Archangel and three views of the tomb chamber where a marble slab covers the rock of the Sepulchre.

Coptic Chapel. At the rear of the aedicula of the Holy Sepulchre is the small Coptic Chapel. The Copts are Egyptian Christians (the name comes from the Arabic Quft, meaning Egypt) who follow the Monophysitic doctrine that was condemned by the Council of Chalcedon (451). The Coptic church recognizes only the divine and not the human nature of Christ.

The Coptic Chapel in the rear of the Aedicula of the Holy Sepulchre.

The Greek Choir, or Katholicon with the grand iconostasis and altar.

Greek Choir. In front of the aedicula of the Holy Sepulchre is the Greek Choir, which stands on the site of the Katholicon, or Choir of the Canons of the Holy Sepulchre of the crusader period. It takes up practically the entire central portion of the church and is almost a separate place. A grandiose iconostasis at the top of a few steps divides it into two parts: one for services and one for the congregation.

According to ancient tradition, the "omphalos" (umbelicus or center) of the world is located beneath the dome of the transept.

The chamber believed to be the tomb of Joseph of Arimathea and the Holy Prison, an old jail adjacent to the Forum of Hadrian's Jerusalem.

The **Tomb of Joseph of Arimathea**, which is reached via the Syrian-Orthodox Jacobite chapel is a rock-carved Jewish tomb dating from the era of Christ. Therefore, it is real evidence that the area was used for burials and was located beyond the city walls, and thus offers some proof of the authenticity of the Holy Sepulchre.

Holy Prison. This small room, also known as Christ's Prison was part of older buildings that stood on the site. The name came into common usage in the VII century and refers to the night Jesus spent in jail after his arrest in the Garden of Gethsemane. It is widely believed, however, that the room is visible evidence of an ancient prison attached to the Forum of the Aelia Capitolina.

The Crypt of Saint Helena. The crypt, situated in an awe-inspiring setting is named after the mother of Constantine the Great and commemorates her efforts to find the Holy Places which led to the discovery of the True Cross and Jesus' tomb. The crypt has a dome dating from the crusades (XII century) which is supported by four XI century columns. Today the chapel belongs to the Armenian church. On the roof of the chapel are the cells of the Ethiopian or Abyssinian monastery; the Ethiopian Church is also monophysitic.

The Crypt of Saint Helena and the stairs leading down.

On the following pages, a view of the crypt and details of the church.

THE MURISTAN AND
THE LUTHERAN CHURCH
OF THE REDEEMER

Just a short distance from the Church of the Holy Sepulchre is the **Muristan** (which means hospital in Persian). Here Charlemagne built a complex that included a church, monastery and pilgrims' hospice which was destroyed by the caliph Al-Hakim. Shortly after the year 1000, merchants from Amalfi built two hospices. The church of one, dedicated to **St. John the Baptist,** still stands. It was built over the earlier church, and dating from 450 is the oldest in Jerusalem. During the crusades it became the seat of the Sovereign and Military Order of the Knights Hospitaller of St. John of Jerusalem, also known as The Knights of St. John of Jerusalem. Although even Saladin kept it alive, the area gradually went into decline. In 1869 the Turkish government gave part to the Greek patriarchate and part to Prussia which built the lovely **Lutheran Church of the Redeemer.** The building encompasses the remains of the Medieval church of Santa Maria Latina. The apses, cloister, columns and a beautiful door decorated with the signs of the zodiac and symbols of the months are visible. Much of Muristan is taken up by a Greek bazaar, that enlivens the whole district. In the middle of the bazaar is the Mora Fountain, near the site of the ancient church of Saint Mary Minor now known as Saint Mary Major.

On these two pages, the Lutheran Church of the Redeemer the Mora Fountain and the colorful shops in the Muristan.

The **Latin** (Roman Catholic) **Patriarchate** of Jerusalem is located north of the Jaffa Gate. It is easily recognized by its triangular façade: a stone plaque commemorates the visit of Pope Paul VI on 6 January 1964 during his historic journey to the Holy Land.

East of the Latin Patriarchate we come to the "Greek" part of the Christian Quarter. Here we find the **Museum of the Greek Orthodox Patrarichate** in a building that dates back to the crusades. The museum contains many archeological relics from different periods, Paleochristian engravings, Roman and Byzantine glass. Along with incunabula and manuscripts there is also a copy of the Edict issued by the Caliph Omar in 683 confirming Christians' rights to the holy places in the city.

The **Anglican Christ Church** stands practically on the edge of the Armenian quarter near the Citadel. It is the oldest protestant church in the Middle East, built in 1830 in the Neo-Gothic style. The building adjacent to the church used to be the British consul's residence.

The church of the Latin Patriarchate of Jerusalem and two views of the Greek section in the Christian Quarter.

The Anglican Christ Church and a panorama of the quarter with the Church of the Redeemer and the domes of the Holy Sepulchre

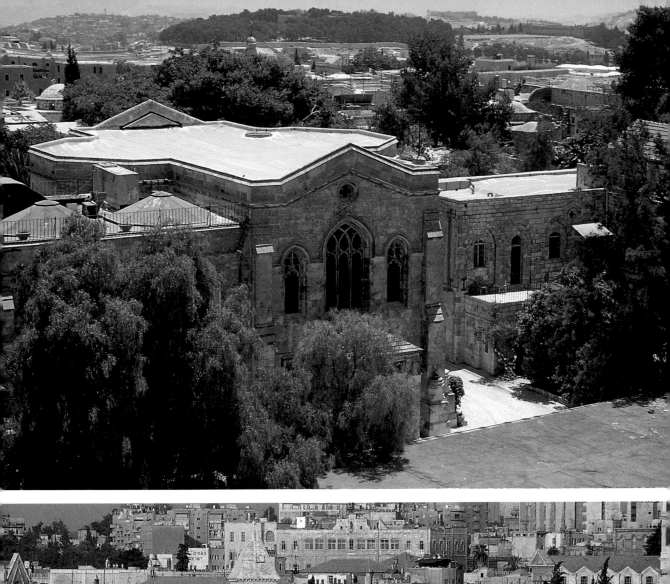

THE MUSLIM QUARTER

This is the largest, liveliest, most colorful and chaotic of the four quarters comprising the Old City, crowded with tourists and pilgrims nearly every day of the year. In addition to its unmistakably Oriental markets it offers visitors monuments of Islamic art which, unfortunately, are not always in the best condition or repair. Some corners preserve the ancient features of Mamluk building techniques and are true, and unfortunately very rare, examples of a Medieval Arab city. The symbol of the Muslim Quarter (and even of the city itself) is the Mosque of Omar. Its great gilded dome, and unforgettable shape stand out against Jerusalem's skyline, or rather, against the sky of El-Kuds, The Holy, as it is called by Muslims.

The mosques on the Temple Esplanade and the Damascus Gate as seen by David Roberts.

The elegant outlines of the Mosque of Omar against the Jerusalem sky at sunset.

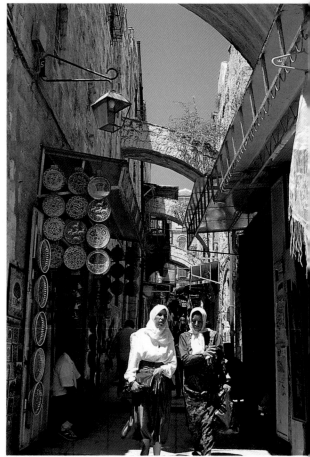

Lively alleyways and streets in the Muslim Quarter.

The magnificent Damascus gate seen from inside and outside the city.

In addition to foods and objects that you can find at markets anywhere in the world, the Jerusalem **souk** (Arabic for market) also sells wide varieties of seeds and spices. Their bright colors, and mainly their unusual and penetrating fragrances, create an indelible memory for many visitors. Fabrics, handcrafted pewter, silver, copper, brass and leathergoods, Armenian and Yemenite jewelry, pottery and rugs, as well as an enormous selection of souvenirs, headdresses and local costumes, favorites with tourists, are displayed inside and outside the shops, along the narrow streets that wind over the nearly flattened hills of the Old City.

The **Damascus Gate**, a stupendous example of Ottoman architecture, and an outstanding blend of elegance and defensive structures, leads into the lively Muslim district from the north. It is flanked by two towers and crowned by a decorative motif that seems to lighten its massive bulk. It stands over the site of earlier gates built by Herod Agrippa and Hadrian, remains of which have been uncovered by archeological excavations.

The souk on Friday, the Muslim day of rest; one of the many minarets in the city's skyline, and a part of the Muslim quarter.

The people of Jerusalem in traditional and modern clothes walking along the city streets.

An interesting example of Mamluk architecture is the **Souk el-Qattanin**, the indoor market of the cotton merchants which also has two Turkish baths. Much of the charm of the Muslim Quarter, and of the whole city, comes from the people. Whether dressed in traditional costumes or modern clothing, they are intent on their work, indifferent to the crowds of pilgrims and tourists who swarm through the streets looking for places, memories, monuments and, of course, souvenirs.

THE TEMPLE ESPLANADE

At the peak of what has been identified as the biblical Mount Moriah stretches the huge artificial esplanade that preserves the memory of the second Temple erected by Herod the Great and destroyed by Titus' legions.
This large area that extends over about 12 hectares is in an uneven rectangle, partially bounded by massive walls.

It is a holy place for all three monotheistic religions.
For Christians it recalls two important moments during the life of Christ; for Jews it is the place where Abraham brought his son Isaac to sacrifice, and mainly because it was the site of Solomon's Temple, and the Second Temple. At the same time it is a holy place for Muslims.

The Temple Esplanade with the mosques as seen from the south; the Ophel Archeological Garden is at the base of the southern wall of the Haram.

their third place of pilgrimage after Mecca and Medina. The excavations in the **Ophel Archeological Garden** next to the southern wall of the esplanade have brought to light the large double door, which is walled over and partly covered by Crusader buildings. It was the gate leading out of the Temple Compound, while the entrance, the Triple Door, reached by stairs as well, was over to the right. Among the various finds there is the ritual bath ("mik-vah"), recognizable by its double staircase, an "impure" side for going down into and a "pure" side for coming up after the ritual. Remains of Byzantine and Omayyad buildings have also been found: the Omayyad palaces stood next to the southern wall. An ancient city gate, from the era of the First Temple was discovered near the street (Derekh ha-Ophel) that flanks the Archeological Garden.

The Mosque of Omar and the elegant south portico.

The gilded dome seems to rest on one of the porticoes crowning the staircase.

THE MOSQUE OF OMAR

In 640 the caliph Omar ibn al-Khattab built the first square-shaped mosque, but in 687 Abd al-Malik ibn Marwan, caliph of the Omayyad dynasty, replaced it with a building of incomparable beauty, the **Qubbat es-Sakhrah** or, the **Dome of the Rock** (which is incorrectly, but universally, called the Mosque of Omar).

In the XII century it was transformed into a Christian church called Templum Domini, but it was returned to the Muslim faith by Saladin in 1187. It rises in the large, rectangular enclosure known as Haram esh-Sharif (The Noble Enclosure) on a platform reached by four impressive staircases that culminate in elegant, colonnaded porticoes known as "mawazim" that is, scales, because according to Islam, scales to weigh souls will be hung on the Day of Judgement. Thanks to its position it is visible to all, and from all sides. The building is an octagon and all its sides are finely decorated; the four sides that correspond to the compass points each have doors with porticoes. The splendid dome in the center of the octagon was entirely gilded by the caliph Abd al-Malik.

On these pages, details of the polychrome decorations on the outside of the Mosque of Omar, and the mosque.

The exterior has two overlapping layers of decorations: below, a colored marble band, and above, blue faience tiles with arabesques that Suleiman the Magnificent had made at Kashan in Persia to replace the mosaics of the previous decorations. The marble band is also a replica of the original sixteenth century decoration. The pediment was embellished in 1876 with an inscription praising the glories of Allah; the work was done by the famous Turkish calligrapher, Mohammed Chafid.

The stupendous gold mosaics inside the dome, and a detail of the interior of the mosque.

The interior with the two rows of marble columns and pillars encircling the sacred rock.

The interior is divided by a double colonnade of 12 pillars and 28 monolithic columns made of fine marbles taken from Christian churches destroyed by the Sassanian invasion in 614, and by the balustrade that encircles the rock sacred to both Jews and Muslims. One legend tells us that the rock wanted to follow the prophet on his way to heaven, but the Archangel Gabriel stopped it and left the imprint of his hand. A few steps lead to the grotto below the rock. The Muslims call it the "Well of the Souls": they believe that all souls will meet there on Judgement Day.

The interior of the building, illuminated by 36 windows is finely decorated throughout.

The cupola, in particular, is covered with gold and plaster decorations. Light filters through windows and the air is filled with the fragrances of tamarisk and jasmine oil burning in the censers, and of the aromatic compound known as "khulik" spread daily on the rock to create an atmosphere that would give the faithful a taste of Paradise as they walked around the rotunda.

The Mosque of Omar with a detail of the Qadi Burhan ed-Din Minbar in the foreground.

A detail with two of the windows on the building's octagonal base, and the dome between the arches at the top of one of the staircases.

ISLAMIC ART

Off to the side of the southern staircase leading to the Dome of the Rock, there is a richly carved marble structure named for its builder. It is the **Minbar** (cathedra) **of Qadì Burhan ed-Din**. Opposite the eastern entrance to the Dome of the Rock, and inspired by its architectural lines is the **Qubbat es-Silsileh** or, Dome of the Chain, it was built by Abd al-Malik to house the treasure of the Haram. Another interesting building is the **Qubbat el-Miraj** or Dome of the Ascension on the northwest. It is here that the Prophet Mohammed is said to have prayed before going up to heaven; during the crusader period it was used as a baptistery.

North of this building there are some smaller structures such as the **Qubbat el-Arwah**. Other structures including

Koran schools and fountains dot the Haram.

The **Gate of the Chain**, Bâb es-Silsileh, stands against Wilson's Arch, with its interesting two domes. The muezzin calls the faithful to prayer from the minaret five times a day: "God is great. There is no other god but God. Mohammed is his prophet... Come to prayer; come to salvation. God is Great. There is no other god but God." Next to the Gate of the Chain is a splendid example of Mamluk architecture: the **Madrasah el-Ashrafiyya**, built in 1482.

The **el-Kas** (meaning the bowl) fountain stands between the staircase and the Al Aqsa Mosque, and it is normally used for ablutions prior to prayer. The **Sebil Qait Bey** fountain (named after the Mamluk sultan who built it) is

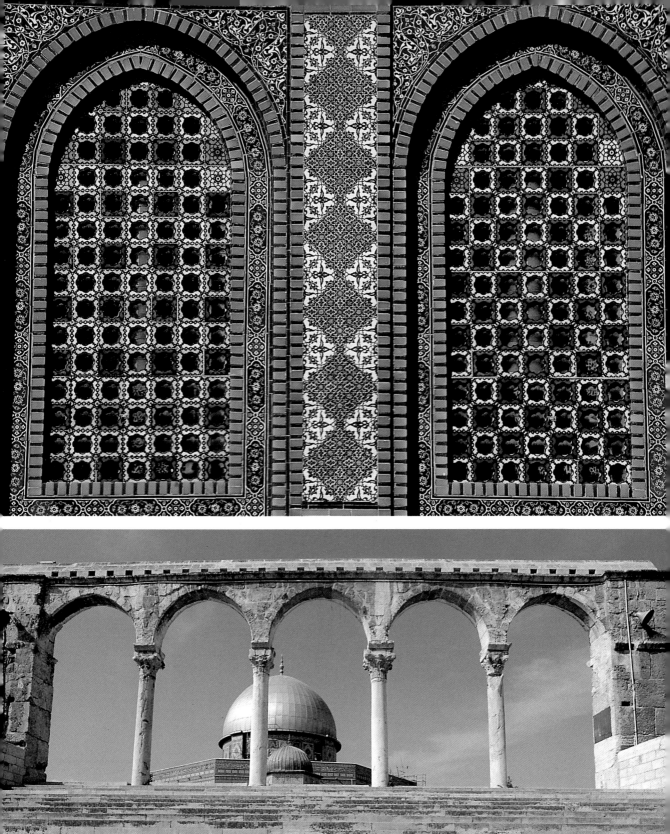

Some of the buildings around the Mosque of Omar;
the Bab es Silsileh with the Qait Bey fountain, a lovely
edicula and a detail of the fountain.

Two impressive views of the mosque.

near the western staircase that leads up to the Dome of
the Rock. It is square-shaped and surmounted by a dome.
And according to one tradition it stands over the site of
the Holy of Holies of the Herodian Temple. A third fountain, **Sebil es-Sultan Suleiman** is located on the northern
side of the Haram near another graceful building, the
Qubbat Suleiman. To the east, near the Golden Gate is
the **Kursi Suleiman** (throne) from which, according to
legend, King Solomon watched the construction of the
First Temple. The **Golden Gate,** bricked over at some
unknown date, owes its name to an error. It was actually
called "Oraia" (meaning beautiful in Greek) (Acts 3,1-8).
This was the gate which, from the Atrium of the Gentiles
within the Temple Enclosure, led to the Atrium of the
Women. Therefore, it was not an entrance to the enclosure, but was inside it. Then an incorrect interpretation of
the Greek text led to the Latin rendition of "aurea" because it sounded so like the Greek word. It is also known
as the Gate of Mercy by the Muslims who prefer to be
buried nearby because the Koran (sura 57,13) links this
door or gate with Allah's last judgement.

THE AL-AQSA MOSQUE

The name means "the farthest" because, according to the Muslim tradition, it is the farthest point to which Mohammed went. The building dates from 709-715 when the caliph Walid I had it built over the foundations of Solomon's palace. The original building had 280 columns arranged in 14 rows, but it was completely destroyed by three earthquakes. It was enlarged by the Templars who came to Jerusalem in 1099. At the end of the XIII century, after the Mamluks drove out the Christians it became the Al Aqsa Mosque, 90 meters long and 60 meters wide.

The mosque has a silver dome and a low façade; the portico has seven

The façade and magnificent interior of the al-Aqsa Mosque.

The central nave of the mosque. the floor is covered with rugs.

The shining dome of the al Aqsa Mosque, the home of the Islamic Museum, and a carved capital outside the entrance to the Museum.

arches that repeat the interior arrangement of seven naves. The columns supporting the interior arches are made of Carrara marble donated by Mussolini on the occasion of the restoration work done between 1938 and 1943, at the same time, King Farouk of Egypt donated the ceiling.

King Abdullah of Jordan was assassinated in here on 20 July 1951, and his grandson, the current King Hussein escaped the same fate thanks to a heavy decoration he was wearing on his chest. The bullet marks are still visible on one of the columns.

In 1969 a deranged visitor set a fire inside the mosque so that lengthy restorations and repairs had to be undertaken

The Islamic Museum. It is located at the southeastern corner of the esplanade. It displays items of various provenance including votive offerings, lamps, and weapons. There is also an interesting collection of manuscripts and a beautiful Mamluk Koran.

Solomon's Stables. This name, a product of pure fantasy, is used to designate the huge underground area at the southeast corner of the esplanade. The room, with its ceiling supported by pillars arranged in twelve parallel rows, was built by Herod to compensate for the difference in height between the Temple Mount and the Kidron Valley below so that the huge esplanade could be constructed. The Templars used this chamber to stable their horses and camels.

West of the stables a staircase (now bricked over) led to the Triple Door. The southeast corner of the Haram has been identified as the **Pinnacle of the Temple**, the site of Jesus' temptations as described in the Gospels. The view from here is superb: the gaze can travel from the Mount of Olives to Gethsemane, from the Kidron Valley to the village of Siloah.

The southwest corner of the Haram and Solomon's Stables.

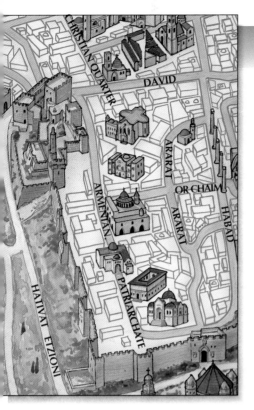

THE ARMENIAN QUARTER

On the southern side of the wall, the **Zion Gate**, built in 1540, slightly to the west of the Roman gate that marked the end of the Cardo, leads into the Armenian Quarter in the southwestern part of the Old City. It is a very distinctive district and is practically an island unto itself as it is inhabited only by Armenians whose ancestors probably arrived at the time of the Roman conquest (I cent.B.C.). The presence of an Armenian community in Jerusalem was already documented in the V century A.D., and up to the XX century comprised only religious congregations; today there are lay families as well.

Beyond the gate we come to the **Armenian Seminary** and the **House of Annas**, father-in-law to Caiaphas. Actually, it is the Church of the Archangels and dates from about 1300. The area adjacent to the western section of the walls, up to where Herod's palace stood is known as the Armenian Garden and is bounded on the east by the street that runs under the arches of the building that houses the seat of the **Armenian Patriarchate**. The Armenians were the first nation, in antiquity, to embrace Christianity (301) through the efforts of St. Gregory the Illuminator. Actually, there are two branches of the Armenian church, the Catholic and the Gregorian which is Monophysitic.

Opposite page, the Zion Gate and the Armenian Seminary; below, the seat of the Armenian Patriarchate.

During its history, the Armenian people whose home is in the region that borders between Turkey and the Armenian Republic, like the Jews, suffered diaspora, persecution and extermination. What the Ottoman empire perpetrated against the Armenians in Turkey is considered the first episode of scientific genocide. The quarter is structured like a monastery-fortress, probably because of the conditions these people had to endure during the XIX and XX centuries.

The first floor of the **Armenian Museum** presents an exhaustive overview of this peoples' history, the genocide and the community in Jerusalem. On the second floor are archeological finds from excavations in the quarter and objects of Armenian art: pottery, sacred vestments, religious items, valuable illuminated manuscripts and the old printing works. Armenian writing was born in the V century A.D. with the development of its own alphabet.

THE CATHEDRAL OF ST. JAMES

This is one of the most beautiful churches in Jerusalem. It was built by crusaders and Armenians in the XII century on the site of a Georgian monastery. The interior of the building is divided into three naves by four pillars that support the drum of the dome. It is filled with paintings, decorations and other items typical of Armenian churches.

Interior and exterior views of the Chapel of St. James.

Two views of the interior, with the choir and Cathedra of St. James.

The dome with its forest of lamps, and a lateral chapel.

A forest of oil lamps hangs from the ceiling, the floor is covered with rugs, the doors and wooden wall panels are carved, gilded and inlaid with mother-of-pearl.

In the choir, a very old chair is known as the Cathedra of St. James; the faithful believe that the apostle used to preach from that seat. Two of the four chapels on the north wall date from the V century. One is the **Chapel of St. Menas**, an Egyptian martyr, where the cathedral treasure and fine manuscripts are kept. The other is the **Chapel of St. James**. On the opposite side is the **Chapel of Etchimiazin** where there are three stones: from Mount Sinai, Mount Tabor and from Jordan. It stands over the site of the narthex of the church that was closed down in the XVII century.

The Church of St. Mark.

The Church of St. Mark. From Ararat Street, which recalls the name of the mountain in Armenia where Noah's ark is said to have landed after the Flood, we reach the small Syrian-Jacobite district which consists essentially of the Monastery and Church of St. Mark. It is believed that the church stands over the site of the house of Mary, mother of Mark the Evangelist, where St. Peter sought refuge after his miraculous release from prison. The members of this congregation also believe that this was the site of the Last Supper.

The Syrian-Jacobites, who call themselves "orthodox" get their name from Jacob Baradai who, in 543 founded this Monophysite community in Syria, thus breaking away from the Church of Antioch that had accepted the Council of Chalcedon. In Syrian-Jacobite churches there is always an evangelistary in front of the altar.

The Armenian Seminary and the site of the house of Mary, mother of Mark the Evangelist; today there stands the Church of St. Mark.

The entrance and two views of the interior of the Church of St. Mark that belongs to the Syrian Jacobite congregation

THE CITY OUTSIDE THE WALLS

MOUNT ZION

HA-OPHEL

VALLEY OF KIDRON

MOUNT OF OLIVES

BEYOND THE DAMASCUS GATE

BEYOND THE JAFFA GATE

MOUNT ZION

Outside the **Zion Gate** is the hill which, since the IV century A.D., has erroneously been called Mount Zion. Originally, Zion was the Jebusite fortress on Mount Ophel. After it was conquered by David it became known as the City of David. According to tradition, the **House of Caiaphas** the High Priest stood in what is now the cemetery of the Armenian patriarchs.

THE DORMITION ABBEY

This massive structure that rises on Mount Zion resembles a mighty fortress; it is topped by a high, domed bell-tower, a conical dome and corner towers. The church, built over the site where the Virgin is said to have fallen asleep for the last time, is the last in a series of buildings erected here over the centuries. It was completed by Kaiser Wilhelm II during the first decade of the XX century based on plans by Heinrich Renard, based on the model of the Carolingian cathedral of Aix-la-Chapelle. The church belongs to the Benedictines. The highlights are the mosaic and the wood-and-ivory statue of the sleeping Virgin in the crypt.

The Zion Gate and the Dormition Abbey.

The outside, a chapel and the crypt with the statue of the sleeping Virgin Mary.

DAVID'S TOMB

The fact that Mount Zion had incorrectly been identified as the site of the Jebusite fortress led generations to believe that King David was buried here (royal tombs, however, have been discovered southwest of the Gihon springs at the foot of Mount Ophel).

The large and venerated sarcophagus is preserved in a crusader period building, erected on the site of an earlier, perhaps primitive Judeo-Christian place of worship. During the XV century the Muslims, who consider David a great prophet, took over this cenotaph and in 1524 they transformed it into a mosque. The room before the tomb chamber is now a synagogue; Christians identify it as the place of the Washing of the Feet.

Between 1948 and 1967 when the Jews were denied access to the Wailing Wall which was in Jordanian hands, they came here on pilgrimage, to pray at David's tomb. The entire building, is currently the property of the State

The outside of King David's Tomb, with the minaret and the Tomb.

Two views of the Room of the Cenacle with the mihrab next to a window on the southern wall.

of Israel; the upper floor is the Room of the Cenacle. Outside we can see the old Franciscan cloister; when the monks arrived in 1333 they built the adjacent monastery. Going through the cloister we come to the **Chamber of the Martyrs at King David's Tomb** in memory of the Jewish communities that were wiped out by the Nazis.

THE CENACLE

The Room of the Cenacle, which is entered via the Dormition Abbey is located above David's Tomb. The three columns that divide it into two naves, the pillars, the arches, the window columns and all the Gothic style architectural elements date the room in the XIV century. This room had also been transformed into a mosque, as evident from the mihrab (the niche indicating the direction of Mecca for prayers), against the southern wall. This room was the scene of events recounted in the Gospels: it is where the Eucharist was established during the Last Supper, where the resurrected Jesus appeared before the Apostles on Pentecost. This episode is commemorated in the **Chapel of the Descent of the Holy Spirit**, exactly above the room containing David's Tomb.

The Church of St. Peter in Gallicantu. The name of this church recalls the episode in which Peter denied Jesus three times before the "cock crowed". This church was consecrated in 1931 and belongs to the Catholic Assumptionists, and was built over the remains of an older Byzantine basilica. It has been said, but never officially confirmed, that it stands over the house of the High Priest Caiaphas.

The church crypt has a series of grottoes, one of which has been called Jesus' prison. It is said that after having been questioned by Caiaphas he spent the night here, before being taken before Pontius Pilate.

The Hasmonean Staircase. The name of this staircase probably refers to the era in which it was built. Its ancient stone steps are visible in the garden of the Church of St. Peter in Gallicantu. The staircase connected the residential districts of the High City that extended north of Mount Zion and the Kidron Valley. It was definitely in use during the Gospel era, and it is likely that Jesus descended these steps on the evening of Holy Thursday as he went to pray in the Garden of Gethsemane.

The Hasmonean Staircase and the Church of St. Peter in Gallicantu.

HA-OPHEL

Ha-Ophel is the area that extends from the southern wall of the Temple esplanade to the Pool of Shiloah, and is bounded on the west by the Kidron Valley. It was the original site of the Jebusite city (the biblical fortress of Zion that became the City of David). It is precisely here that archeologists have uncovered the oldest vestiges of Jerusalem, dating from the Bronze Age, with traces of the Canaanite settlement.

A visit to the **City of David Archeological Garden** allows us to trace the long history of the site. There is a stepped-stone structure from the Jebusite period (perhaps part of the Fortress of Zion), the remains of a house burned during Nebuchadnezzar's siege (586 B.C.), a segment of wall rebuilt by Nehemiah and the ruins of a Hasmonean tower. Following the Bible's indications, on this site were discovered several tombs, one of which might be the tomb of King David.

The Gihon Spring and the Pool of Shiloah. The ancient city's water supply system is particularly interesting. For centuries the **Gihon Spring,** the only natural resource, was located outside the Jebusite walls. To avoid leaving the city, the early inhabitants made use of a natural tunnel passing below the city walls, which led to **Warren's Shaft** (named after its discoverer) from which the water of the spring could be drawn. Due to its steepness, steps were carved in the rock of the first part of the tunnel, which lead to the top of the shaft. It was through this route that King David managed to enter the city and conquer it.

In the VIII century B.C. the king Hezekiah, foreseeing that the Assyrian king Sennacherib would besiege the city, built a 500 meter long tunnel, **Hezekiah's Tunnel**, to carry water to the **Pool of Shiloah**. He then ordered the Gihon Spring camouflaged so that the enemy would not find it. The digging was started at opposite ends, the two crews met near the middle of the tunnel. A plaque, engraved in ancient Hebrew, commemorating the event was found in the tunnel about 6 meters from the Pool of Shiloah. The original is in Istanbul but a replica can be seen in the Israel Museum in Jerusalem.

The tunnel is not straight; its winding path may have been developed because of ventilation or the rock structure. It has a slight gradient of only 0.4% (that is 40 centimeters every 100 meters); its height varies from 1.10 meters to 3.40 meters, and its initial width of 1 meter gradually narrows towards the middle.

The Pool of Shiloah is located at the point where the Kidron and Tyropeion valleys meet. Jesus' miraculous cure of the blind man took place here at the Pool of Shiloah. The Byzantines built a basilica over the pool to mark the event, however it was destroyed by the Persians. The columns that can be seen in the water date from Roman times.

The Pool of Shiloah and the Gihon Spring that gave the city its water.

THE KIDRON VALLEY

Just a glance at the Kidron Valley from the road that runs below the Temple esplanade is sufficient for an understanding of how this place influenced the people of Jerusalem since its earliest days. The barren landscape, the unusual tombs carved into the rock or set amongst the olive trees give it an unreal atmosphere. Popular tradition maintains that the dead will be resurrected here on Judgement Day. History, on the other hand, tells us that even if they are called the Tombs of the Prophets, these unusual burial places date from the Hasmonean period. Here is the **Tomb of Jehoshaphat**, of **St. James** (actually this is the tomb of the Bnei Hezir, a family of priests, the name means "sons of Hezir) with the architrave resting on two columns, and the pyramid-shaped **Tomb of Zechariah. Absalom's Pillar** also called the "pharaohs crown" because of its cone-shaped upper part, dates from the period of the Second Temple, and recalls David's rebellious son who "...in his lifetime had taken and reared up for himself a pillar, which is in the king's dale: for he said, I have no son to keep my name in remembrance and he called the pillar after his own name, and it is called unto this day, Absalom's place" (2 Samuel, 18:18).

Absalom's Pillar and the Kidron Valley with the Tombs of St. James and Zechariah.

The Church of All Nations

THE MOUNT OF OLIVES

The Mount of Olives rises beyond the Kidron Valley which separates it from the Temple hill. It is particularly important to Christians, since Jesus crossed its slopes many times as he went to Jericho and Bethany.
The little Greeek Orthodox **Church of Viri Galilei** commemorates the resurrected Jesus' descent on the Apostles.

The Garden of Gethsemane. It is one of Christianity's great holy places. The fact that even today there grow ancient, gnarled olive trees has stoked the belief that they may be the same trees that witnessed Jesus' last night before his arrest. In Hebrew Gethsemane (Gat Shemanim) means oil press, and evidently refers to the many olive trees growing there.

The **Grotto of Gethsemane** which is supposed to be where Jesus, betrayed by Judas, was arrested, is just a short distance from the Church of the Tomb of the Virgin. Notwithstanding restoration work done during the nineteen fifties, of all the holy places in Jerusalem, the Grotto of Gethsemane has best maintained its original appearance, that is, the way it looked in the days when Jesus walked the earth. From the VI century on the place which had been used as silo for a nearby estate, was used as a Cenacle by some Christian congregations.
Inside the cave, with its interesting stone ceiling, there are three altars each of which has murals above it. Above the main altar is a portrayal of Jesus praying with the Apostles; the paintings above the lateral altars depict the Assumption of the Virgin and Judas' kiss.

The Church of All Nations on the slopes of the Mount of Olives.

The Garden with its ancient olive trees, the Grotto of Gethsemane believed to be where Jesus was arrested.

ATIONESQVE CVM CLAMORE VA

SQVE

The Church of All Nations, details and the façade.

On the following pages, the rock where Jesus is said to have prayed, details of the domed ceiling and two mosaics.

THE CHURCH OF ALL NATIONS

In the idyllic setting of Gethsemane, one of the most impressive places in all Jerusalem, stands the church built by the Italian architect Antonio Barluzzi (1919-1924). The church, also known as the Basilica of the Agony in reference to the night Jesus spent here on the eve of his Passion, combines the architectural lines of Christian basilicas (the façade) with the salient features of Islamic buildings (the sides and roof with many little domes). The name, Church of All Nations is dedicated to all the countries that contributed to its construction.
The insignias of those nations decorate the little domes, which give the entire building a decidedly Oriental air. A Byzantine church was built on this site in the IV century, and later the crusaders transformed into in a basilica.
The façade, enclosed by an elegant wrought iron gate is reached by a flight of steps. An array of columns supports the three big arches that mark off the atrium, while the tympanum is decorated with a modern mosaic depicting Jesus as the link between God and mankind. Inside, some fragments of mosaic flooring are evidence of the ancient Byzantine church.
The most outstanding element is in the presbytry where, before the main altar, we can see a huge fragment of rock on which Jesus is said to have prayed on the eve of the Passion.
The rock is surrounded by a wrought iron crown of thorns. In the apse there is a mosaic depicting the agony of Christ, who is consoled by an angel. Other mosaics in the lateral apses portray other episodes from the Passion, such as Judas' kiss, and Jesus' arrest.

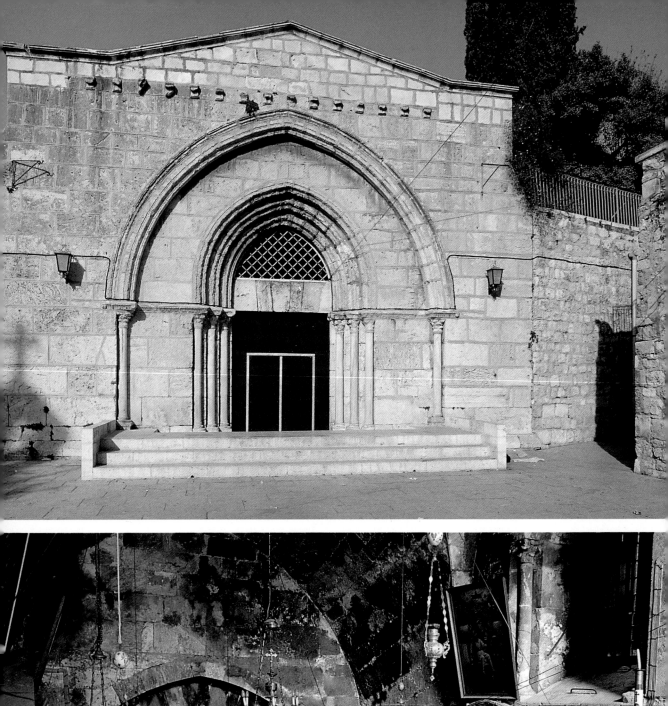

The austere, crusader façade of the church and the stairs leading down to the Tomb of the Virgin.

The burial chamber, with the altar and the rock where the Virgin's body rested.

The Church of the Tomb of the Virgin. Also known as the Church of the Assumption, the building carries the lines of the XI century restorations done by the crusaders. Its origins date from the Byzantine era (V century), and the crypt, carved into the rock, is the most significant religious point of interest in the church.
Stairs lead to the underground burial chamber, where the **Tomb of the Virgin** is visible in the center, surrounded by paintings, magnificent icons and lamps. Although this church has claims to be Mary's tomb, it must be remembered that there is another Tomb of the Virgin at Ephesus in Turkey, where Mary is said to have been taken by the Apostle John. Going down the stairs into the crypt, on the right we see the Tomb of Queen Melisend, daughter of Baldwin II, King of Jerusalem) which has been transformed into a chapel and dedicated to Saints Joachim and Anne, the Virgin's parents, and on the left, the chapel dedicated to Saint Joseph.

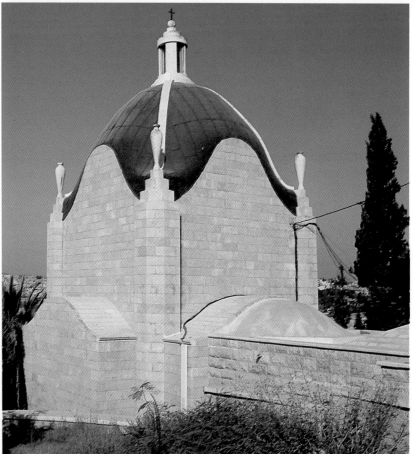

The city seen from the window above the altar in the Church of Dominus Flevit, and the dome of the church.

The dome of the Church of Saint Mary Magdalene with the Church of All Nations in the foreground.

The Church of Dominus Flevit. This Franciscan church was built by Antonio Barluzzi during the nineteen thirties over the ruins of a V century structure. Recently, traces of a necropolis were found here, with several funerary inscriptions in Greek, Hebrew and Aramic. The window above the altar offers an incomparable view of Jerusalem. The church's name means "the Lord wept". Before entering Jerusalem Jesus stopped to cry over the fate that awaited the city. "...And shall lay thee even with the ground, and thy children within thee; and they shall not leave in thee one stone upon another; because thou knewest not the time of thy visitation" (Luke 19:44).

The Church of Saint Mary Magdalene with its typical gilded domes.

Two views of the interior of Saint Mary Magdalene.

THE CHURCH OF ST. MARY MAGDALENE

The Church of Saint Mary Magdalene stands out against the skyline with its distinctively Muscovite architecture, seven gilded onion-domes topped by crosses. The building, nestled on the western side of the Mount of Olives was built in 1885 by order of Tzar Alexander III in memory of his mother, Maria Alexandrovna.

Inside there are several fine paintings, icons and the tomb of the grand duchess, Elizabetta Fyodorovna, who was assassinated during the Russian Revolution in 1917.

The Russian Tower and the top of the Mount of Olives,
and the Basilica of the Sacred Heart with the Cloister
of the Pater Noster.

The Cloister and the Lord's Prayer in different languages

The Russian Tower. An outstanding feature of th
panorama of the Mount of Olives is the Russian Tower
the slim spire of a Russian monastery. One of its rooms
that has been made into a museum, has a beautiful mosa
ic floor with an Armenian inscription; it may well dat
from the VI century, and it was part of an Armenia
monastery.

The Cloister of the Pater Noster. Near the area of th
old Basilica Eleona built by Saint Helena, mother of th
emperor Constantine, today stands the Basilica of th
Sacred Heart, built in 1920. Adjacent to the basilica is th
Cloister of the Pater Noster, as this is the site where Jesu
taught his disciples the Lord's Prayer. There are 44 ce
ramic tiles on the walls: each one inscribed with th
Lord's Prayer in a different language.

143

The Aedicula of the Ascension, its surrounding wall and the rock conserved in the chapel.

Jerusalem from the Mount of Olives, and the dromedary, a must for tourist snapshots. On the following pages, the roofs and domes of the old city, with the modern city in the background.

THE AEDICULA
OF THE ASCENSION

According to the Gospel, forty days after the Resurrection, Jesus appeared before his disciples and led them to the Mount of Olives and "...while he blessed them, he was parted from them, and carried up into heaven". This is where Jesus' life on earth ended; here the supernatural event is commemorated by a chapel which since the XIII century belongs to the Muslims who consider Jesus one of the great prophets. The building has been markedly changed with respect to the original structure which had a double, circular portico and open arches. Inside the aedicula is the rock with a footprint said to have been left by Christ as he ascended to heaven.

BEYOND THE DAMASCUS GATE

The **Damascus Gate** on the northern side of the walls enclosing the Old City opens onto a part of Jerusalem with many interesting places and monuments.

Just a few hundred meters from the gate are **King Solomon's Quarries** that were probably used during the era of the First Temple to provide building stones. It is a complex network of tunnels also known as the **Grotto of Zedekiah**, according to one legend, King Zedekiah fled from the Babylonians via these tunnels.

Another nearby cave is the **Grotto of Jeremiah**, once again, according to legend, the prophet came here to weep when Jerusalem was destroyed by the Assyrians.

Near the Prophets' Street (Rehov ha-Nevi'im) is an **Armenian Funeral Chapel** also known as the **Church of Saint Polyeuctos**, that houses one of the most beautiful mosaics in all Israel: about forty different birds arranged on a winding vine. The ancient Armenian inscription reads: "To the memory and salvation of the souls of all those Armenians whose names are known only to God". The mosaic, 7.5 by 4.5 meters, dates from the VI century.

Aerial view of the Damascus Gate and the constant crowds going in and out.

148

THE GARDEN TOMB

This place is also known as Gordon's Calvary after the English officer who discovered this site from atop the Damascus gate. It is a rocky place, surrounded by a garden, with an ancient tomb that many Christians believe to be the real sepulchre of Christ. Seen from different angles, the hill is indeed shaped like skull. Furthermore, other features, such as a large cistern, wine press and its position near the city gate, have led many to consider it a valid alternative to the other Holy Sepulchre. The atmosphere is so serene and tranquil that it inspires prayer and meditation.

This site is cared for by the Garden Tomb Association with headquarters in England.

The Garden Tomb.

St. Stephen's Basilica and a detail of the interior.

The Tombs of the Kings and the huge courtyard
carved into the rock.

St. Stephen's Basilica. This church rises over the traditional site of the saint's martyrdom. Dedicated in 1900, the church was built by French Dominicans on land they had purchased and where they conducted archeological excavations. The fifth century empress Eudocia wanted a monastery dedicated to the saint built here, and also wanted it as her burial place. After the destruction wreaked by the Persians in 614, a small church was built over the site; it was restored by the crusaders who later themselves destroyed it to prevent it from falling into Saladin's hands.

Tombs of the Kings. Notwithstanding the name, these tombs have nothing to do with the kings of Irael who, according to the Bible, are buried in the City of David, that is, on Mount Ophel. On the basis of archeologist evidence this enormous complex of tombs, that belongs to the French government, dates back to the era of the First Temple. A flight of steps leads to a courtyard carved into the rock where two lateral channels carried rainwater to two underground cisterns. The courtyard had a portico with columns, and some traces of the original decorations are still visible. The cave-tomb complex has a large room that leads to the burial chambers. In four of these, along the walls, are burial benches complete with headrests carved into the stone. The innermost chamber, reached by few steps, contains a sarcophagus carved out of the living rock.

Exterior and interior views of the Anglican Cathedral of St. George.

Two of the tombs discovered in the Sanhedriya Park, they are known as the Tombs of the Sanhedrin or Tombs of the Judges.

The Anglican Cathedral of St. George. A short distance from the Tombs of the Kings stands the Anglican Cathedral of St. George, with its distinctive four-spired tower. The church was built at the end of the nineteenth century, but the architecture is highly reminiscent of Oxford University.

Tombs of the Sanhedrin or Tombs of the Judges. The Sanhedriya Park, in the district of the same name, is one of the loveliest spots in the city. It includes a large necropolis with rock-carved tombs on three different levels, dating from as many different periods. Some are from the Hasmonean era and others date from Herod's day. The sculptures on some of the tombs are clearly of Hellenistic inspiration with columns, pillars and acanthus leafed friezes. Tradition did not allow the names of the dead to be put on the tombs, to prevent famous people from being worshipped as gods by later generations, so it is difficult to ascertain actually who is buried here. Tradition holds that, in addition to the prophet Samuel, members of the Sanhedrin from the Second Temple period are interred here.

The Rockefeller Museum, with its distinctive towers,
and one of the rooms.

Two of the museum display rooms with objects from
various periods and places.

THE ROCKEFELLER MUSEUM

Also known as the Museum of Archeology of the Holy
Land, this museum was made possible thanks to a be-
quest by the American industrialist and philanthropist,
John Davison Rockefeller; it was built by the English architect Austin Harrison and decorated by Eric Gill. It is
an elegant white and pink stone structure, with an octagonal tower. The exhibit rooms open onto a pool encircled
by a portico.
It is located on the area where Godfrey of Bouillon
pitched his camp before launching the final attack on
Jerusalem. The rooms contain archeological finds dating
from the Paleolithic Period to the Crusades. Obviously,
there is a wide variety of objects on display: from coins
to pottery, from jewels to weapons, from sculptures to illuminated Korans, to Judaic antiquities. In the courtyard
with the pool, there are several sarcophagi, and fragments
of columns and capitals.

Two views of the former Italian Hospital.

The Italian Hospital. Although it is now the headquarters of the Ministry of Culture and Education, this building is still known as the Italian Hospital. Its Neogothic lines recall a famous Italian monument: Palazzo Comunale in Siena with the Torre del Mangia, and this may be another reason that the original name has remained in use for so long.

The Ethiopian Church. This round, late nineteenth century building was erected by Menelik, emperor of Ethiopia. On the façade is the Lion of Judaea, symbol of the Empire. According to tradition, the Queen of Sheba came from Ethiopia, when King Solomon welcomed her in Jerusalem. He gave her a lion.

Me'a She'arim. This is the ultraorthodox Jewish district: the people who live here scrupulously follow the Law and Jewish tradition. Long beards, black clothes and hats for the men, skirts that reach below the knees, long sleeves for women (married women cover their heads) are all the distinctive signs of these people. If you want to visit this district that abounds with synagogues and yeshivot (Talmudic schools) you must dress modestly and above all, avoid going between sunset on Friday and Saturday. Life practically comes to a halt on the Sabbath which is dedicated to prayer.

The Russian Cathedral. Green domes, topped by gold crosses, characterize the Russian Orthodox Cathedral of Jerusalem. A huge, twelve-meter long column lies on the ground in front of the cathedral. It may have broken during the construction of Herod's Temple. During the British Mandate in Palestine, the English authorities had occupied part of the monastery and turned it into offices. The church stands on the site known as the Field of the Assyrians. It seems that Sennacherib's troops camped here in preparation for their seige of the city. Then, centuries later, Titus' armies camped in the same place when they destroyed the Temple.

The Russian Cathedral is easily recognized by its beautiful green domes.

BEYOND THE JAFFA GATE

Outside the **Jaffa Gate**, before reaching the new part of Jerusalem where the government ministries, the Parliament and the city's most prestigious cultural institutions are located, there are several interesting historical and archeological sites to see.

To the south, beyond Mount Zion, is the **Valley of Hinnom** (the biblical Gehenna) of bitter fame. The point where it converges with the Kidron Valley was probably the location of **Topheth** where human sacrifices were made in honor of the god Molochi mentioned in the Second Book of Kings and the Second Book of Chronicles.

The **Hakeldama** (field of blood in Aramaic) is also in this area. Tradition says that it was purchased with Judas Iscariot's thirty pieces of silver. The elegantly constructed tombs date from the era of the second Temple, and one is probably the burial place of the High Priest Annas, father-in-law to Caiaphas.

The slopes of the **Hill of Evil Council** (it is said that Caiaphas's country house, where the members of the Sanhedrin met to discuss Jesus' fate, was located here), which creates the valley's southern border, has a large necropolis with tombs dating to the Jebusite period. Those from the Hellenistic period are decorated, and during the Christian era they provided shelter for monks and hermits. The **Greek Orthodox Monastery of Saint Honofrius** is dedicated to one of these hermits. The monastery dates from the XIX century. Another contribution, albeit entirely different, to this valley's "bad" reputation comes from the fact that many foul smelling activities, such as tanning hide, used to be carried out near the Roghel spring.

Northwest of the Jaffa Gate is the large, rectangular **Mamilla Pool**, 60 by 90 meters and 8 meters deep. The bodies of Christians killed during the Persian invasion were thrown here, and this period provides the first account of the existence of the pool. Today part of the pool area is surrounded by a large Muslim cemetery. It is adjacent to the **Independence Park**. The annual Israeli Independence Day celebrations are held here in May.

Hutzot ha-Yotzer, the Center for the Arts and Crafts deserves a little note. It was specially created to acquaint visitors with local craft products. Different types of wares are made in the workshops, from mosaics to sculptures, from gold and silver, to woven cloths, and they are displayed in a dedicated gallery.

The area near the walls and the Jaffa Gate, with the Sultan's pool.

The Sultan's Pool and Suleiman's Fountain.

Suleiman's Pool. It is the name given by the Arabs, in honor of Suleiman the Magnificent, that designates the city's largest (169 meters long by 86 meters wide) cistern outside the Jaffa Gate. Actually, it was built long before the Ottoman period. In fact it is believed that it may be the "dragon well" that Nehemiah (V century B.C.) mentioned in the reconnaissance tour he made of Jerusalem. The enormous basin was later enlarged by the crusaders. Suleiman had it reinforced, gave it its current shape, and built the beautiful fountain which stands on the bridge. An inscription tells us the builder's name and the date: 1536. Today, the drained pool is an outdoor theater, the Merril Hassenfeld Amphitheater.

Mishkenot Sha'ananim (Dwellings of Serenity) is the name of the complex comprising the low buildings overlooking the sultan's pool. It is the first Jewish neighborhood built outside the walls. In 1858 the English philanthropist, (who originally came from Livorno, Italy) Sir Moses Montefiore, created it to solve the problem of overcrowding in the Jewish Quarter of the Old City. Currently, the district houses an art and cultural center.

159

Yemin Moshe. This small district was created toward the end of the XIX century on land that Sir Moses Montefiore had purchased years before. Named after him, the district also includes Mishkenot Sha'anaim, one of the city's best residential areas.

The Montefiore Windmill. This structure, which has become one of the symbols of Jerusalem stands in the heart of Yemin Moshe. Sir Moses Montefiore built the windmill; it was never very successful and today it is a museum.

The Y.M.C.A. The headquarters of the Young Men's Christian Association was built in 1933 by the same architect who designed New York's Empire State Building. The 50 meter high tower offers a stupendous view of Jerusalem. The Y.M.C.A. is an important cultural center with a library, auditorium, movie theater, hostel and a small museum of antiquities.

Herods' Tombs. A big round stone closed the vestibule with its white marble-covered walls, that leads to the three burial chambers. One of the chambers contained two sarcophagi. The elegance and luxury of the tomb has led to the belief that members of the royal family were buried here.

The Yemin Moshe district and the King David Hotel.

The Montefiore Windmill, the Y.M.C.A. and Herods' Tomb

Jason's Tomb. This rock-carved tomb is located in the elegant residential secton of Rehavia and it looks like a small mausoleum. It has a courtyard, and is crowned by a small pyramid; the opening has a central column that supports the architrave. The interior, comprising a vestibule and two burial chambers has yielded inscriptions with the name Jason and carvings of a battle between two ships and a crouching deer, which date the tomb in the Hasmonean period. It is believed that it belonged to a rich family and was used for several generations. Then it was reused in the I century A.D., as confirmed by coins found at the site. The graffito menora (seven-branched candlestick) on the plaster dates from the same period.

The Great Synagogue. This is the largest and most modern synagogue in all Israel. Nearby stands the synagogue of the Central Rabbinate, or the Heikhal Shlomo, the supreme religious authority which combines the services of the two main Jewish rites, the Sefardic and Ashkenazi. There is also a beautiful XVIII century ark from Padua (Italy) inside. The Museum, known as Dor va-Dor, contains a replica of an old Italian synagogue.

Jason's Tomb and the inside of the Great Synagogue.

Details of the stained glass window in the Great Synagogue.

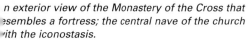

n exterior view of the Monastery of the Cross that
*esembles a fortress; the central nave of the church
ith the iconostasis.

wo interior views of the church.

he Monastery of the Cross. Completely surrounded by
igh walls, this monastery resembles a fortress rather
an a place to live a life dedicated to prayer and medita-
on. However, we must remember that as late as the XIX
entury there was desert beyond the walls of Jerusalem,
nd that meant danger. The monastery was built in the XI
entury by a king of Georgia for the Georgian congrega-
on residing in Jerusalem. The site had been occupied by
V century church and became the property of the Greek
rthodox congregation. Currently it is closed. Both con-
ruction and its name are linked to a legend, depicted on
e walls behind the altar. This is where the tree that gave
e wood for Jesus' cross was cut down. The tree, accord-
g to the legend, had been planted by Adam, cared for
y Abraham, watered by Lot and partially used by
olomon to build the Temple. Pillars divided the church
to three naves; the pavement has fine mosaics with ani-
al figures, and the walls are frescoed with saints. There
only one small door in the outer walls, which leads into
shaded courtyard. Inside are the monks cells.

THE MODERN CITY

THE NEW JERUSALEM

ISRAEL MUSEUM, JERUSALEM

The Knesset Building and the new City Hall.

THE NEW JERUSALEM

Modern architecture in Jerusalem dates from the last thirty years of the nineteenth century, even though the first district beyond the walls was built by Sir Moses Montefiore in 1860. By the beginning of the twentieth century, there were already close to seventy neighborhoods outside the Old City's walls.

The British Mandate left Jerusalem several town plans, and quite a number of unique buildings. The most noteworthy of these include the Rockefeller Museum and the High Commissioner's residence, both designed by the architect Austin Harrison.

Few innovations were made as regards Jerusalem's architecture in the 'fifties and 'sixties. The only original creation, the mushroom-shaped synagogue on the Givat Ram campus of the Hebrew University (Heinz Rau and David Resnick), stood in splendid isolation for many years. The new Givat Ram campus of the Hebrew University was designed in the International Style: as a series of single cubic buildings surrounded by lawns. Eliezer Brutzkus was the planner, and the building designers included Jaski and Alexandroni, Resnick, Rau and David Anatol Brutzkus. Klarvin drew up neoclassical plans for the Knesset building and in the early 'seventies Al Mansfeld designed the Israel Museum taking his inspiration from Arab villages and the casbah. During more or less the same period the Nadlers designed the theater combining traditional Jerusalem stone with modern materials such as glass and cement. Yehiel Shemi, the sculptor, worked on this project which can be considered a

final tribute to Bauhaus architecture, with Mendelsohnian eloquent influences (the same Mendelsohn who designed several of the Mount Scopus campus buildings in the 'eighties before moving to the United States).

The big revolution, however, took place in 1967, the year that it was finally possible to see and be influenced by the ancient architectural treasures of the Old City. The generations of young architects emerged during these two decades came into contact, for the first time, with the architecture of an earlier period. These arches, domes and vaults were a revelation. They were fascinated by the harmony of the language spoken by the stones and the openings in the old walls. Many new districts were built in the ensuing decades such as Ramot Eshkol, Gilo, Armon ha-Natziv, Ramot, and Neve Yakov. They are distinguished by a new approach to townplanning, public and private areas, and traffic lanes are separated from areas created for people alone. The typical round buildings with green courtyards of these districts recall the monasteries, cloisters and mosques found all over the Mediterranean basin. In other parts of these same districts, there are shaded porticoes, perfect for keeping out of the rain or hot sun, and these too, evoke old Mediterranean towns in a modern key.

Other features from the past in these new districts are the terraced buildings and casbahs: the old, familiar lexicon of the Judaean hills is brilliantly rendered in modern form. Examples are the terraced complex designed by Eldar Sharon that winds along a ridge in Gilo, and the

The Bank of Israel.

The Sherover Theater of Jerusalem and the Menorah near the Knesseth.

terraces on the hillside designed by Giora Laufenfeld in another part of the same district. Terraced buildings reach their apex in Hacker's complex in the Ramot district.

A certain number of public buildings were also constructed during the 'eighties and represent an achievement for public architecture in Jerusalem. Some of the major points of interest are the Bank of Israel building designed by Eldar Sharon, inspired by the Boston Town Hall; the She'altiel Community Center in the Armon ha-Natziv district is a rather extravagant example of public architecture in this period. The sculptor Matteus Görietz and the architects Spektor and Amissar created a functional structure which is also a sculpture. The building resembles a group of polyhedrons that form a plastic composition. Moshe Safdie designed the final part of the Hebrew Union College complex (that had been started by H. Rau).

During the 'seventies, the Hadassah Hospital on Mount Scopus originally designed by Erich Mendelsohn in the 'thirties was completed in the International Style by Rechter and Zarchi while maintaining the nature of the original plans. An eminently plastic solution was adopted for the Hebrew University Campus on Mount Scopus. There were already some buildings from the 'twenties,

including the National Library designed by Patrick Geddes and Chaikin, and this was supplemented by Carmi's grandiose contemporary building. The new campus designed something like a casbah, fortified on the outside, with a series of internal courtyards that should provide inspiration and favour intellectual activities.

At the end of the 'eighties Carmi and Carmi designed one of the most sensational structures in all Jerusalem: the Supreme Court building, inspired by Harrison's nearby Rockefeller Museum. The building is decidedly modern, characterized by open spaces that offer glimpses of the sorroundings, and wise use of the natural lighting in the courtrooms and big lobby. The inner courtyards are circled by porticoes with Jerusalem stone roofs creating a sense of peace for all those who move around in this building.

Another design that raised a storm of controversy in the late 'seventies and early 'eighties was the Moshe Safdie concept for the plaza at the Wailing Wall; much of the work remained unfinished. He had planned an arched structure with terraces sloping downwards from the Jewish Quarter to the plaza at the Wailing Wall, a sort of terraced casbah with low arches, arched windows and glass and stone domes. Only the Porat Yosef Yeshiva

168

was completed, and not even this fulfilled the architect's intentions.

Another design by Moshe Safdie is the impressive Mamilla complex comprising residential units inspired by casbahs, decorated with small plastic domes, and commercial premises, or rather a business-tourist center that reaches from the City Hall to the eastern end of the Jaffa Road to the Jaffa Gate. In the Mamilla Project Safdie rediscovered the city's pre-Bauhaus architectural style, with its porticoes, galleries, upper and lower roads alongside of considerable commercial space and stores. Construction is still underway. Only after it is completed will it be possible to grasp the architectural significance of this prestigious project.

The new Jerusalem City Hall, designed by Diamond, Kaulker and Epstein is compact and very formal, taking up three sides of a square, and it vaguely recalls the lictorian or fascist style. This building stands between older ones dating from the British Mandate, and together they create an interesting complex. It surrounds the Daniel Auster Park gracing the main entrance to the City Hall. The building was inaugurated at the end of 1993.

The first tall buildings -not quite skyscrapers- in Jerusalem, hotels, office or residential buildings date from the 'eighties and include the Hilton Hotel (today the Holiday Inn), the Eilon Tower and the City Tower. Skyscraper construction was halted in the 'eighties under pressure from then-mayor Teddy Kollek who was concerned about the effect they would have on the city's appearance. The administration of the young, dynamic mayor Ehud Olmert will go down in history as the era of the return to multi-storey construction.

The fact that Jerusalem cannot expand to the east, north or south makes it necessary to turn "inward" for growth. The sacrosanct principles of the British Mandate that prohibited construction of tall buildings in the valleys will not be fully respected. The city will indeed enter a new architectural era. However the still open question is: will the town planners be able to preserve most of the unique nature of Ottoman and Mandatary Jerusalem? Or will we witness a gradual change in the appearance, atmosphere and nature of this very special city?

Arch. DAVID CASSUTO
DEPUTY MAYOR OF JERUSALEM

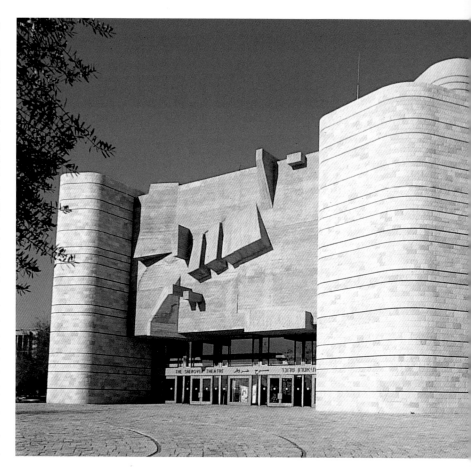

ISRAEL MUSEUM, JERUSALEM

This museum, designed by the Israeli architects, Alfred Mansfeld and Dora Gad was opened in 1965. Its modern pavillions fit in well with the green landscape dotted by olive and cypress trees.

The museum is divided into five sections: the Bronfman Biblical and Archeological Museum; the Bezalel Art Museum; the Billy Rose Sculpture Garden; the Ruth Youth Wing; and the Shrine of the Book, which illustrates the three great periods of Jewish history and culture: the Biblical period, the two thousand years of the Diaspora and the modern State of Israel.

The first period is presented through a rich exhibition of items related to the peoples and cultures of the Holy Land and the surrounding regions. These people had engaged in cultural and economic exchanges since the earliest times. From prehistory to the beginning of the Muslim conquest, daily life, art, funeral rituals and religion (the monotheistic faith of the Jews and later of the Byzantines, the polytheistic religions of the Canaanites, Philistines, Phoenicians, Greeks and Romans) are richly illustrated by the items unearthed during archeological excavations in the area.

The second period, The Diaspora, is represented by ethnographic collections portraying daily life, work, the clothing and jewels of various rural and urban Jewish communities scattered throughout the world. There are also manuscripts and religious objects that reveal the cultural affinities with the countries where these communities were established.

The Fine Arts Collections contain drawings, prints and paintings by foreign and Israeli artists dating from the XV to the XX century. This collection forms the link be-

Bible scrolls on display in one of the museum's rooms. Ivory figurines from Calcolithic period (second half of the IV millenium B.C.), and anthropomorphic sarcophagi showing clear Egyptian influence; the sarcophagi were found at Deir el-Balah (XIII century B.C.).

The Israel Museum with the Monastery of the Cross in the foreground.

Chanukah menorahs from various periods and places, and the trousseau of a Jewish bride from Buhara.

Detail of the coin gallery, and a floor mosaic from a Roman villa (III century A.D.)

tween past and present, with works by great artists including Cranach, Rembrandt, Monet, Cézanne, Matisse, Schiele, Chagall, Picasso, Rothko and Kiefer.

There is more space for the present: the Billy Rose Sculpture Garden is dedicated to contemporary sculpture and contains pieces by Rodin, Maillol, Picasso, Moore, Marini, Wotruba, Vasarely and Turrel just to list the most famous names, as well as works by Israeli artists. Also Departments of design, photography, Tribal and pre-Columbian art, Far Eastern art, European period rooms.

The Ruth Youth Wing is a very special place. It has its own exhibition gallery, and studios for the study of plastic arts; it also has a theatrical and multimedia workshop that opens the doors to the future for its thousands of young members.

Statue of a seated youth with a jaguar's head on his stomach (Precolombian art, 600-900 A.D.), and " Two Girls in Nice" by Henry Matisse, oil on canvas (1921).

The Israel Museum, with its dual exhibition-educational structure is a vital cultural center. Knowledge of the past merges with experimental activities to provide cultural and social enrichment for its members and visitors Jewish and Muslim children, adults who want to learn more, and erudite scholars from all over the world find a wealth of information, here, as well as a starting point for their own cultural development and experimentation, in various cultural fields.

Exterior and interior views of the Shrine of the Book where the famous Dead Sea Scrolls are carefully kept.

THE SHRINE OF THE BOOK

This section of the museum contains the famous Dead Sea Scrolls, two-thousand year old manuscripts that were discovered in terracotta jars in caves at Qumran.

The pavilion housing the scrolls was designed by the American team of Frederick Kiesler and Armand Bartos. It has a dome shaped like the covers of the jars found at Qumran, while the contrast between the white dome and the black basalt wall alludes to the dualistic concept of the cosmos divided between Light and Darkness, and the triumph of the Sons of Light over the Sons of Darkness. Only the white dome is visible from the outside since the structure is almost entirely underground. It is reached by a tunnel that leads to the circular room where the manuscripts are displayed. One of the most important scrolls found at Qumran is seven meters long: it contains the Book of Isaiah, and is the most ancient Jewish manuscript known today. Other scrolls deal with the rules of the Dead Sea Community, a sect that withdrew to the desert to live in strict observance of Mosaic Law.

AROUND THE CITY

EIN KEREM

MOUNT HERZL

THE HILL OF REMEMBRANCE

BETHLEHEM

EIN KEREM

Although it is never mentioned in the Gospel, Chrisitan traditions and literary sources maintain that the village of Ein Karem (source of the vine in Hebrew) was the birth-place of John the Baptist. Archeological discoveries have in part substantiated this tradition.

The Sanctuary of St. John the Baptist. The sanctuary, which is in the hands of the Franciscan order, dates from the end of the XIX century. The earlier crusader building was destroyed by Saladin who turned it into a cara-vanserai. The three-nave church houses some fine orna-ments. At the end of the left nave, a flight of steps leads down into a natural cave which is believed to have been part of Zachary's house: hence the tradition that it was Saint John's birthplace. The site of the sanctuary also contains evidence of previous eras. In 1885 a chapel with two Roman tombs and a mosaic with Greek inscriptions attributing the tombs to Christian martyrs was found under the portico. Later, another chapel with a mosaic floor was discovered adjacent to the first, and below both there was a press from the Roman period. Next to the second chapel, steps led down to a grotto that contains vessels from the Herodian period; and finally, a statue of Venus was found in the courtyard in front of the church.

View of Ein Karem with the Sanctuary of Saint John the Baptist.

Interior views of the sanctuary and the crypt.

The Church of the Visitation. This church, nestled on a rocky hillside, shaded by cypress trees is also known as the Church of the Magnificat in memory of Mary's reply to her cousin Elizabeth during the Gospel episode of the Visitation. The famous hymn to the Lord, the Magnificat, is given in 41 languages on one wall of the church. The existing building belongs to the Franciscan order and was completed between 1938 and 1955 to designs by the Italian architect, Antonio Barluzzi.

Remains of previous places of worship were uncovered during construction. Two highlights are traces of a Byzantine church and another built by the crusaders in the XII century. The building consists of two parts: religious services are held in the Upper Church. In the crypt there is a grotto where water gushed from a miraculous spring when Elizabeth welcomed the Virgin. Other curiosities include a stone against a wall bearing the imprint of a boy's body. Tradition tells us that the imprint was left by the young St. John when Elizabeth hid him from Herod's soldiers during the Slaughter of the Innocents.

The Church of the Visitation seen from the outside, and the Virgin Mary portrayed on the façade.

Interior views and the words of the Magnificant on one wall

The Hadassah Medical Center. One of the most beautiful artworks of our day can be seen in the village of Ein Karem: Marc Chagall's stained glass windows in the Hadassah Medical Center Synagogue, inaugurated in 1961. The 12 windows depict the 12 sons of the Patriarch Jacob, from whom the 12 tribes of Israel are descended. Each window is a different color, on the basis of the description of the High Priest's pectoral in the Book of Exodus. With the cooperation of his assistant, Charles Marq, Chagall developed a special technique that allowed him to use as many as three colors in each panel; earlier techniques required lead separations between each piece of glass.

The Synagogue at the Hadassah Medical Center with the magnificent stained glass windows by Marc Chagall.

MOUNT HERZL

...e highest peak in Jerusalem is dedicated to the memo-
...of Theodor Herzl (1860-1904) founder of Zionism, the
...ovement that promoted the Jews' return to their ances-
...l land from the various parts of the world in which they
...re scattered. Many famous Zionists and former Israeli
...ime ministers such as Golda Meir and Itzhak Rabin are
...so buried here.

...erzl's Tomb. A square granite slab in the middle of the
...uare has held the mortal remains of Theodor Herzl
...ce 1949. In accordance with his last wishes, the
...under of Zionism was buried at the top of this mount,
...if to symbolically watch over Jerusalem, heart of the
...ate he had envisaged. He had asked to be buried in
...enna until the day the Jewish people could move his
...mains to the land of his fathers.

...he Herzl Museum. This small museum contains the
...dy of the Hungarian journalist and writer, reconstruct-
...with his books, letters, papers and personal objects.

*...eodore Herzl's Tomb and the Museum dedicated to the
...under of Zionism.*

THE HILL OF REMEMBRANCE

A journey to Jerusalem is not complete without a visit to the Har Ha-Zikaron, the Hill of Remembrance: a complex of buildings and monuments dedicated to the victims of the Holocaust, the Shoà. It is a memorial to the six million Jews exterminated by the Nazi madness, but it is also a reminder to the living of "what happened" as Primo Levi said in his book *"Se Questo E' Un Uomo"* (Survival in Auschwitz).

YAD VA-SHEM

The name, which in Hebrew means a Place and Name, was taken from the Prophet Isaiah (56:5). A visit here leaves a lasting and disturbing impression, but it is important and advisable. There is the **Wall of the Shoà and Heroism,** a monument by Naftali Bezem. The panels commemorate the extermination, celebrate the Resistance of the Jewish Partisans and illustrate the survivors' return to the land of their fathers. Two other sculptures by Nathan Rapaport are dedicated to **The Last March to Annihilation** and the **Warsaw Ghetto Uprising.** The **Janusz Korszak memorial** honors the Polish educator.

The flame and a detail of the Ohel Yizkor.

who did not want to abandon his pupils and followed them to the Treblinka camp. The **Museum** contains documents, photographs and writing that provide a broad picture of Nazism from its inception to the end, and of the "final solution of the Jewish problem" in Europe. Then there is the **Ohel Yizkor** (Hall of Remembrance): a low, reinforced concrete structure on a basalt base; the pavement is simply inscribed with the names of twenty-one main death camps. In one corner, below a flame that is relit at 11:00 a.m. every morning with a brief ceremony, there is an urn containing human ashes taken from a crematorium oven. The **Children's Memorial** commemorates the one and half million children who"went up the chimneys" of the crematorium ovens; the names in the **Valley of the Destroyed Communities** perpetuate the names of Jewish communities that were entirely annihilated; the **Hall of the Names** contains the names of over two million victims (the list is incomplete because all traces of the others have been lost), and the names of the heroes of the Resistance; The **Avenue of the Righteous** honors all those non-Jews who risked their own lives to save the lives of Jewish friends, neighbors and even total strangers. Their names are carved into stones shaded by trees, the symbols of life. The entire complex is dominated by the **Pillar of Heroism** that is visible from every part of the complex, it is engraved with one word, Zachor: Remember!

Two of the monuments dedicated to the victims of Nazi persecution and to the heroes of the resistance.

Rachel's Tomb, from the outside, and the interior.

Rachel's Tomb. On the road to Bethlehem, just a few kilometers from Jerusalem there is a small building with a white dome that houses Rachel's tomb. As opposed to the patriarchs, Abraham, Isaac and Jacob, and the matriarchs, Sarah, Rebecca and Leah who were all buried at Hebron in the Machpela grotto, Rachel was interred here, where she died giving birth to Benjamin. "And Rachel died and was buried in the way to Ephrath, which is Bethlehem. And Jacob set a pillar upon her grave; that is the pillar of Rachel's grave unto this day" (Genesis 35: 19-20).

BETHLEHEM

Just south of Jerusalem, in the midst of a rural setting which has remained practically unchanged over the centuries, with its Biblical features and nature intact, stands Bethlehem the sparkling little village set against the bleak, rocky hills, where the landscape is dotted with olive and cypress trees. Bethlehem means "the house of bread" from the Hebrew "Beit Lehem", or "house of meat" according to the Arabic ""beit Lahm". This city, holy to Christianity, is permeated with biblical memories and the Gospel.

Even today, shepherds bring their sheep and goats to graze in the pastures, wearing more or less the same dark robes and head coverings as they did two thousand years ago.

The birth of Jesus (Jeshua in Hebrew) left an indelible mark on the history of mankind. The story of Christ's days on earth, this man with a dual nature, human and divine, left an immortal message which even today—on the threshold of the third millenium—affects a vast portion of universal beliefs, thought and conscience. There is, however, no universal agreement as to the date of Christ's birth: the Roman Catholics set it on the night of 24 December; the Greek Orthodox date it 6 January, and the Armenians believe that it occurred on 18 January.

Churches, belltowers and minarets characterize the Bethlehem skyline.

THE CHURCH OF THE NATIVITY

The Church of the Nativity stands on a site that has been venerated by pilgrims since the earliest days. In 135 A.D. in an attempt to annihilate the Christians, the emperor Hadrian dedicated the grotto and small grove to the pagan god Adonis. Only Constantine's intervention in 332 made it possible to restore this place so important to Christian tradition and he built the first place of worship. Later, it was embellished and modified by Justinian who also raised the floor and covered the mosaics in Constantine's church. The existing building looks essentially as it did then. It was spared by Khosrow's Persian troops (614) who considered the Magi depicted in the mosaics on the church façade as their ancestors. Omar paid tribute to the church when he went there to pray to the "Mother of the

The low Door of Humility that leads into the Church of the Nativity; the interior of the church with five naves; under the pavement there are visible sections of the mosaic from Constantine's church.

prophet Jesus". During the crusades it was further embellished and two entrances to the grotto were made.
Currently the basilica belongs to the Roman, Greek-Orthodox and Armenian catholic congregations.
The natural stone façade is squeezed between monasteries of different Christian denominations. We enter the basilica through the small Door of Humility (1.2 meters high) so that we have to bend, as if entering a real grotto. Originally, the door must have been higher; it was decided to make it smaller sometime around the XVII century so that the Muslims would not enter the church on horseback. The interior is astounding and grandiose with five naves separated by four rows of red Corinthian columns. Beneath wooden planks we can see sections of the ancient mosaic floor. In the largest nave there are traces of mosaic on gold ground dating around the middle of the XII century, attributed to a certain "Basilius pictor." The mosaics depict the ancestors of Christ and the first seven Ecumenical Councils.

Detail of one of the mosaics in the church and the Grotto of the Nativity inside the church.

The Grotto of Nativity.

The most significant religious and historical site, however, is the Grotto of the Nativity. This small room, partially covered with marble decorations encloses the Altar of the Birth of Christ. The site of the event is marked by a silver star, illluminated by 15 votive lamps that are also made of silver. The inscription on the star reads "Hic de Virgine Maria Jesus Christus natus est - 1717". There are two other altars: the Altar of the Manger where the newborn Babe was placed. According to tradition St. Helena found the original clay manger and replaced it with another made of silver. Opposite is the Altar of the Magi, where the three kings paid homage to the Infant Jesus.

The Grotto of the Nativity with the Altar of the Birth of Christ in the background; the Altar of the Magi in the Catholic oratory to the right of the Grotto.

The Altar of the Birth of Christ, belongs to the Greek Orthodox congregation; the marble slab and silver star commemorate the event.

The Church of St. Catherine. A complex network of grottoes links the Grotto of the Nativity with the Church of Saint Catherine. This place of worship was built by the Franciscans during the second half of the XIX century. The interior, with three naves, has a ceiling with ribbed cross vaults. The church's fame stems from the fact that Midnight Mass on Christmas Eve is celebrated here and broadcast throughout the world on television. In the center of the cloister, which dates from the crusades, there is a column with a statue of Saint Jerome. According to tradition, the saint known and respected for his learning and well versed in Latin, Greek, Hebrew and Aramaic spent the last 35 years of his life (from 385 to 420) in one of the caves here where he worked on his translation of the Bible, the Vulgate.

The Milk Grotto. A Franciscan chapel is built around the grotto in which, according to legend, the Virgin took refuge to nurse the Infant Jesus. The dark stones supposedly turned white as a few drops of the Virgin's milk touched them. The grotto is a place of pilgrimage for Christian and Muslim mothers.

The cloister and façade of the Church of St. Catherine with the statue of St. Jerome; the Milk Grotto, interior and exterior views.

The Church of St. Catherine during the Christmas celebrations.

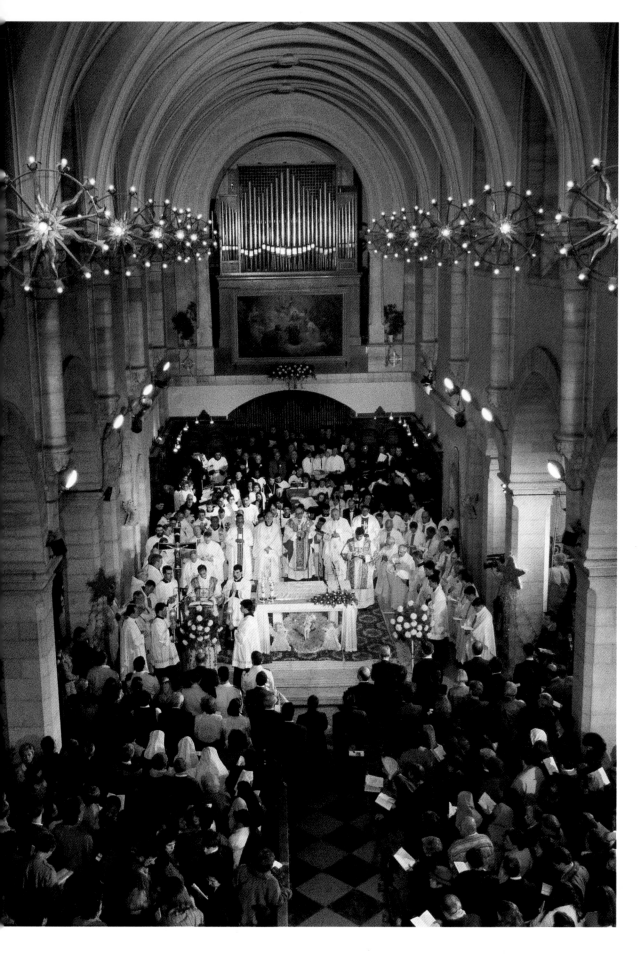

INDEX

ART AND HISTORY OF JERUSALEM
Publication created and designed by Casa Editrice Bonechi
Graphic design and photographic research by Serena de Leonardis
Graphics by Sonia Gottardo
Layout by Studio Forma - Borgo San Lorenzo - Florence
Editing by Rita Bianucci

Text by Rita Bianucci, Giovanna Magi *and* Giuliano Valdes - Editing Studio, Pisa
The New Jerusalem chapter is by David Cassuto, Deputy Mayor of Jerusalem
Translation by Julia Weiss - *Introduction translated by* Studio Comunicare - Florence
Drawings by Stefano Benini *(pages 24, 35, 45, 53, 91, 113) and* Peter Szmuk *(page 70)*

Photographs from the Archives of Casa Editrice Bonechi *taken by*
Paolo Giambone, Garo Nalbandian, Andrea Pistolesi *and* Alessandro Saragosa.
Other photo credits:
Albatross Aerial Photography - Tel Aviv *(pages* 22 - 29 - 41 - 45 - 48 - 49 - 96 - 112 - 148 - 178 top*)*;
Israel Museum - Jerusalem *(pages* 171 bottom left and bottom right - 173 bottom - 174*)*;
Israel Museum/David Harris - Jerusalem *(pages* 171 top - 172 - 173 top - 175 bottom*)*;
Israel Talby - Hadera *(page* 169 top*)*.
The photographs on page 57, courtesy of Kalid Kannan.

ISBN 88-8029-441-5

* * *